Bashabi Fraser is a writer and academic who traverses her two worlds of the sub-continent and Britain. Her publications, which include academic writing, poetry collections, children's literature and edited anthologies, see these worlds converging in books like this one, which she has edited and introduced. Bashabi has a Ph.D. in English and is an Honorary Fellow at the Centre for South Asian Studies at Edinburgh University and an Associate Lecturer in English Literature at The Open University in Scotland and the West Midlands. She lives in Edinburgh with her husband and daughter.

Also by Bashabi Fraser:

Bengal Partition Stories: An Unclosed Chapter (Anthem Press, London, 2005)

Tartan & Turban (Luath Press, Edinburgh, 2004)

Topsy Turvy (Dasgupta and Co., Kolkata, 2004)

JUST One Diwali Night (Dasgupta and Co., Kolkata, 2004)

The Ramayana (Edinburgh Puppet Workshop, 2004)

Rainbow World: Poems from Many Cultures, edited with Debjani Chatterjee (Hodder, London, 2003)

With Best Wishes from Edinburgh (Writers' Workshop, Kolkata, 2001)

Edinburgh: An Intimate City – An Illustrated Anthology of Contemporary Poetry on Edinburgh, edited with Elaine Greig (The City of Edinburgh Council, 2000)

Life (Diehard Publishers, Edinburgh, 1997)

Peoples of Edinburgh: Our Multi-cultural City, edited with Helen Clark and Lorraine Dick (The City of Edinburgh Council, 1996)

*For
Stephen,
With love and warm regards,
Bashabi Fraser.*

To my father Bimalendu Bhattacharya and my former teacher, Professor Kitty Dutta, and, in memory of my mother Anima Bhattacharya.

A MEETING OF TWO MINDS

Geddes Tagore

LETTERS

Edited and introduced by Bashabi Fraser

Word Power Books

43 West Nicolson Street, Edinburgh, EH8 9DB
tel: 0131 662 9112
books@word-power.co.uk
www.word-power.co.uk

COVER SKETCH OF TAGORE BY ROTHENSTEIN courtesy of Marion
Geddes
COVER SKETCH OF PATRICK GEDDES BY AN UNKNOWN INDIAN ARTIST
courtesy of Claire Geddes
PHOTOGRAPHS OF PATRICK GEDDES courtesy of Edinburgh University
Library
PHOTOGRAPHS OF TAGORE, RATHINDRANATH, ANDREWS AND
SHANTINIKETAN courtesy of Rabindra Bhavana
PHOTOGRAPHS OF ARTHUR GEDDES courtesy of Claire Geddes
PHOTOGRAPHS OF MONTPELLIER courtesy of Bashabi Fraser
PICTORIAL POEM BY TAGORE courtesy of Marion Geddes
BACK COVER PHOTOGRAPH OF BASHABI FRASER by David Williams
INTRODUCTION © Bashabi Fraser

FIRST PUBLISHED IN THE UK by Edinburgh University: Edinburgh
Review Book Series, 2002
PUBLISHED IN INDIA by Visva-Bharati University Press, 2004

THIS REVISED EDITION PUBLISHED by Word Power Books, 2005
TYPESET by Govind Kharbanda (www.gokhart.com) in *eff* LondonA
PRINTED AND BOUND IN THE UK by Digisource Ltd.

ISBN 0-9549185-1-7

ACKNOWLEDGEMENTS

I owe this book to the joint co-operation of two institutions in the East and West, who gave their full consent to read and publish the entire correspondence compiled in this book. I would like to thank the Director of The National Library of Scotland and the Adhyaksha (Director) and the Librarian, Supriya Roy of Rabindra-Bhavana (the Archival Centre of Tagore's works), and the Central Library at Visva-Bharati and all the staff at both institutions for their unfailing support and patient assistance. This book would not have been possible without the generous permission granted by Marion Geddes, Patrick Geddes' eldest granddaughter, to use and publish the Geddes correspondence. Marion Geddes' faith in me enabled me to complete this editing task. Both Marion and her sister, Claire Geddes, have very kindly given me the photographs of Arthur Geddes and the sketch of Patrick Geddes by an unknown Indian artist (so appropriate for this book, presenting Geddes as he was known during his Indian period). I am grateful to Professor Swapan Majumdar (Adhyaksha), for encouraging me to use the letters of the entire Tagore-Geddes circle – a brilliant piece of advice – since some letters by Tagore and Geddes are missing/lost, so the ones by other luminaries known to both of them, do fill many of the existing gaps and answer some puzzling questions. This book would have been incomplete without the photographs of Tagore and of Shantiniketan and Sriniketan, for which I am very much obliged to Visva-Bharati.

I would also like to thank the Edinburgh University Library for all its help, and especially the staff of the Special Collection for taking the trouble to sift through the unimaginable mountain of material on and by Geddes and for giving me the photographs of Patrick Geddes to use for this book. I am grateful to the Centre for South Asian Studies, Edinburgh University, for giving me the research position I needed to do this work. I would also like to thank the School of Social Sciences, especially the Department of Sociology, for giving me the office space and administrative backup, without which, I would not have been able to proceed with this research project. In this connection, I would like to mention Professors Roger and Patricia Jeffery, Dr. Crispin Bates, Professor Jonathan Spencer and both the secretaries of Sociology and thank them for their support.

The story of this book is itself a story of Indo-Scottish inspiration and encouragement. I would like to thank Professor Murdo Macdonald for asking me to do something about the Tagore-Geddes correspondence, my former teacher, Professor Kitty Dutta (a Scot who spent most of her teaching life in Bengal), for saying, 'you should do it!' (*i.e.* edit the Tagore-Geddes correspondence), and my friend Rachel Blow, for pointing out that Geddes was off the Rabindra-Bhavana Museum map altogether. The list of people who have helped me is long, of which I can only mention a few such as Sophia Leonard of the Geddes Centre, Professor Iain Boyd Whyte of the Department of Architecture at Edinburgh University, Vivian Rossi of the Scots College at Montpellier, Professor Kalyan Bagchi and Mrs. Bagchi, Professor Pulin Das, Arunendu Banerjee, the Indian architect, Kenny Munro and Leslie May (both sculptors) of the Geddes Association, the teaching staff of the A.J.C. Bose Institute in Kolkata and its Museum Curator, who have, in different ways, been the diverse illuminating forces behind this book – as varied and interesting as the two great men whose letters are the subject of this book.

I would like to thank the staff at the various guest houses at Visva-Bharati, for the hospitality they extended to me during my several visits there. I would also like to thank Professors Kumkum and Ranjit Bhattacharya for providing me a home at Shantiniketan during my research visits there.

Alexandra Wong did the initial, difficult type setting. Sue Renton, secretary of the School of Social Sciences, Edinburgh University, my friends Dr. Tapati and Swapan Gupta and the staff at the Computer Centre, Visva-Bharati, all assisted in the electronic corrections to this book. I am grateful to them and to Rajatsubhra Chakrabarty for his electronic assistance and to Govind Kharbanda for doing the layout of this edition. I would also like to thank Tarlochan Gata-Aura and Elaine Henry at Word Power Books for agreeing to publish this revised edition.

8

My parents first led me to the Patrick Geddes legend, as they knew Arthur Geddes personally. They also gave me the privilege of growing up in a culture enriched by Tagore's presence, which is so alive in the Bengal they brought me back to after their research at the LSE, for which I am eternally grateful. They have read, advised on and clarified many of the details in the Introduction of this book. This work would not have happened without my sense of a new identity, that of being an Indo-Scot, which I owe to my husband, Neil. It has thus become a mission for me to link my two countries, something Tagore and Geddes tried to do, as is evidenced in this correspondence. Without Neil's unstinting help, suggestions and infinite patience, this book would not have been possible. And last, but not the least, this book has as its impetus, my daughter Rupsha's inter-cultural present and future, for whom I want to leave this small legacy, not of Empire and all the misunderstanding such memories entail on both sides, but of understanding and effort, that is possible when like minds meet.

Bashabi Fraser
Edinburgh, July 2005.

Foreword

Murdo Macdonald

It is an honour to write a foreword to this collection of letters exchanged between Patrick Geddes and Rabindranath Tagore. Bashabi Fraser's research gives us significant insight into the relationship between these two contemporaries whose careers bridged the late nineteenth and early twentieth centuries. Fraser's work is the more important because the link with Geddes has been a neglected aspect of Tagore's life, perhaps because Geddes is most remembered today as a pioneering ecologist and town planner, rather than as a cultural activist. Geddes' cultural activism was, of course, inherent to his ecological and planning activities. Tagore understood this very well when he wrote, in the foreword to Geddes' first biography 'he has the precision of the scientist and the vision of a prophet; and at the same time the power of an artist to make his ideas visible through the language of symbols.' Yet the most profound link between Tagore and Geddes was their shared sense of the interdependence of the local, the national and the international. When Lewis Mumford wrote of Patrick Geddes that 'his Scotland embraced Europe and his Europe embraced the world' could he not have written with equal validity of Tagore that his Bengal embraced India and his India embraced the world? For both Geddes and Tagore are characterised by their internationalism, yet for both men this internationalism is based firmly on an understanding of, and utter commitment to, locality.

University of Dundee

November 2001.

Introduction

Leaves are masses of silence
round flowers which are their words

— Rabindranath Tagore

By leaves we live

— Patrick Geddes

… there is neither East nor West, Border, nor Breed nor Birth,
When two strong men stand face to face, though they come from
the ends of the earth!

— Rudyard Kipling, 'The Ballad of East and West' (1889)

INITIAL STEPS

The exchange of ideas and thoughts in the form of letters, which bear testimony to an important friendship between two great men, negates the oft-quoted idea that East and West cannot meet. Resurrecting them has been a daunting task. Nevertheless, compiling and editing the correspondence between Patrick Geddes and Rabindranath Tagore, has proved worthwhile.

After my return from Britain to India, in the early sixties, I grew up in a culture steeped in Tagore, in the language we spoke, catching ourselves quoting Tagore consciously or unconsciously, in our daily speech in the Bengali we spoke (like Shakespeare in English), finding expression for every mood, occasion and festival in his numerous songs (over 2,200), dancing his dance dramas and being confronted by him in the daily rhythm of life in India.

When I came to Britain in the 1980's, I was a witness to Geddes' reconstruction work in Edinburgh, 'There stand the houses he has built – visible, tangible, delectable; concrete proof that he is no visionary'.[1] I was also amazed to see how few knew about Tagore or even remembered him, though he visited the world on invitations and gathered huge audiences when he spoke, in Europe, America and Canada (he also visited the Far East and South East Asia, South America, Iran and Egypt on similar trips). I spoke of him as a poet, a song composer, a novelist, a short story writer, a playwright, an essayist, a painter, a social and rural reformer, a political thinker and philosopher, an environmentalist, an educationist. When the response has been lukewarm, I have found myself being defensive, saying to, sometimes, an almost unbelieving audience, that he had won the Nobel Prize for Literature for his English translation of *Gitanjali* in 1913. It was on this trip, that quite by chance I met Jeannie Geddes, the widow of Arthur Geddes. Mrs. Geddes was a friend of Carmen Dakin, a family friend, with whom I was staying at that time. Jeannie Geddes gave me a set of the songs of Tagore that Arthur Geddes had compiled and edited, with musical notations and English prose translations. It was a strange coincidence, for my parents had known Arthur Geddes back in England, as fellow geographers. In fact, my father recalls that Arthur Geddes had spoken to them in fluent Bengali!

After my return from Edinburgh to India, I was struck by the temporary oblivion Patrick Geddes had suffered even amongst the intelligentsia. *Who was Patrick Geddes?* And again I fumbled – town planner? biologist? architect? sociologist? physicist? generalist[2]? environmentalist? educationist? It is in this last capacity that I wish to

---

[1] Philip Boardman, *Patrick Geddes: Maker of the Future*, Introduction by Lewis Mumford (Chapell Hill, The University of North Carolina Press, 1944), p. 154

[2] Murdo Macdonald refers to the 'untimely generalism' in 'Patrick Geddes – educator, ecologist, visual thinker' in *Edinburgh Review*, Issue 88, Summer, 1992.

introduce both Geddes and Tagore, *i.e.*, by discussing their ideas on Education. For Geddes was, perhaps, one of the most well-known Scots in his time in the world as Tagore was one of the most known Indians outside India (apart from Gandhi or even Nehru and we are not looking at political figures here) – both in the East and the West, known internationally as intellectuals, and seen as representative of their respective countries, Scotland and India.

When I returned to Scotland, it was Professor Murdo Macdonald, then at the Centre for Continuing Education at Edinburgh University,[3] who put me onto this Geddes-Tagore relationship, asking me if I could do something about it. But I hadn't a clue as to what I could or should do. My friend, Rachel Blow, who has a long familial link with Bengal, gave me the next prod I needed. She came back from a trip to Shantiniketan and told me of her dismay when she did not find a single reference to Patrick Geddes at the Rabindra-Bhavana, the archival centre of Tagore's University, Visva-Bharati, to which Geddes had lent a hand in planning. I wanted to know *why*. Why was there this near obliteration from memory of Geddes in India and Tagore in Britain?

Perhaps, one reason behind their present neglect is that the trust and enthusiasm they aroused and nurtured in their lifetime has lost the inspiring spark of their presence. Even while they were alive, we know that their institutions foundered in their absence.[4]

But even while they were alive, there were many times when they were misunderstood and were often lonely souls. 'Much of what I must say about Geddes applies equally, I find, to not a few other men of genius I have known... for in one way or another one must pay for their extraordinary gifts: the very self-absorption that sustains their work, along with

---

[3] The whole concept of continuing education, which is now promulgated by the 'School of Life Long Learning at the Centre for Continuing Education', is so much in line with what Geddes had taken as the initiative to push for from 1887 onwards, in the University Extension Movement in Scotland. Incidentally, Professor Macdonald now holds the chair for Scottish Art History at Dundee University, where Geddes was a Professor (albeit of Botany), when it was part of the University of St. Andrews.

[4] '... projects tended to founder when Geddes himself was not longer totally involved, vitalizing them with his energy...' Paddy Kitchen, *A Most Unsettling Person*, (London, Victor Gollancz Ltd., 1975), p. 17. And similarly, 'In Tagore's absence his institutions tended to go to pieces...' Krishna Dutta and Andrew Robinson, *Rabindranath Tagore, The Myriad-Minded Man*, (Bloomsbury, 1995), p. 275.

a godlike self-confidence, breaks down normal social attachments.'[5] Lewis Mumford, who says this, had not personally known Tagore, but those who did know him, could well apply this passage to Tagore. Tagore was a lonely man in many ways and as Kripalani[6] describes his stand, beliefs and work, his was 'A Lone Voice',[7] that of, as Gandhi shrewdly put it, 'The Great Sentinel', and as Kripalani adds, 'of the rights of man.'[8] The belief that such men are not capable of 'normal social attachments' is a harsh judgement, based on Mumford's initial meeting with Geddes which flawed his later relationship.[9] But this kind of response perhaps explains the ambivalence evident in some of their social and personal relationships and commitments.

Mumford goes on to remark, 'Genius, just because of its originality, tends to be self-isolating; and the less its departures are understood and accepted, the more self-protectively inviolable becomes the resulting solitude, and the more difficult it is to overcome the solecisms that result from this isolation.'[10]

In the course of this book, 'Geddes' will be a reference to Patrick Geddes and 'Tagore' to Rabindranath Tagore. Other Geddeses and Tagores will be specified by use of their full names as in Anna Geddes or Debendranath Tagore. The place, Shantiniketan where Visva-Bharati is, is referred to with an 'Sh'. In the Geddes-Tagore correspondence, we have retained 'Santiniketan', unless otherwise spelt by the writer, *e.g.*, in the letter of 26 February 1926 by Geddes to Mahalanobis and by Arthur Geddes in his later letters. In our references to the place, we will use the 'sh' to denote the labial sound, to differentiate it from the dental 's', to reflect the Bengali phoneme and spelling.

5 *Lewis Mumford and Patrick Geddes: The Correspondence*, ed. and introduction by Frank G. Novak Jr. (London and New York: Routledge, 1995), p. 346.
6 Kripalani was the husband of Nandita, the adopted daughter of Rathindranath Tagore, Rabindranath Tagore's son.
7 Krishna Kripalani, *Rabindranath Tagore: A Biography* (New York: Grove Press Inc., 1962), pp. 356-90
8 Ibid, p. 350.
9 'Somehow, our companionship got off on the wrong foot; and we never managed to fall in step afterward...' Ibid, p. 345.
10 Novak, 1995, ibid.

PEOPLE AND PLACES

Some explanations are necessary at this stage to describe the people and places who/which are important to this correspondence.

Shantiniketan means the abode of peace. It was where Tagore's father, Maharshi[11] Debendranath Tagore meditated one evening under two *chhatim* trees, and taken by the sheer bareness of the place, decided to buy it.[12] This is where Tagore founded his school in 1921. The school became the nucleus from which the poet started on his next ideal, the International University, Visva-Bharati. It was inaugurated in December 1922.[13] Tagore was keen on the idea of a synthesis of the East and West.[14] In 1919, with leading intellectuals in Europe, he had signed 'La déclaration pour l'indépendence de l'esprit', an initiative of Romain Rolland. So later that year, Tagore wrote to Rolland of his deep hurt in seeing how Asia had no real love for Europe as there was contempt on the one side and hatred on the other.[15] It was to make possible and to perpetuate this 'synthesis … the meeting of East and the West'[16] that he established Visva-Bharati, his International University.

In a letter dated 11 October, Rabindranath Tagore wrote to his son, Rathindranath from USA: 'I have in mind to make Santiniketan the connecting thread between India and the world. I have to found a world centre for the study of humanity there. The days of petty nationalism are numbered – let the first step towards universal union occur in the fields of Bolpur. I want to make this place somewhere beyond the limits of nation and geography.'[17] This is something which Geddes too attempted in graphically taking the viewer beyond the Edinburgh skyline to all the

---

[11] Maharshi or the Maha Rishi means the Great Sage, so-called because of his ascetic ideals and the way of life he adopted for himself and for his children.

[12] Dutta and Robinson, p. 53.

[13] Kripalani gives the date as the 23 December (Kripalani, 1962, p. 299), while Dutta and Robinson give it as 22 December, (p. 220), though its foundation stone was laid three years earlier on 22 December, 1918 (ibid).

[14] Dutta and Robinson, 1995, p. 222.

[15] Ibid.

[16] Ibid. In 'A Poet's School' Tagore says '…I refuse to think that the twin spirits of East and West, the Mary and the Martha, can never meet to make perfect the realization of truth. And in spite of our material poverty and the antagonism of time I wait patiently for this meeting.' In Humayun Kabir, *Towards Universal Man: Rabindranath Tagore* (London: Asia Publishing House, 1961), p. 295.

[17] Dutta and Robinson, 1995, p. 20.

continents and the universe beyond at the Outlook Tower.[18]

Arthur Geddes was Patrick Geddes' second son. Arthur himself was a geographer. At his father's wish, he came to Shantiniketan. From 1923 to 1924, he stayed at its sister institution of **Sriniketan**, which is the centre for Rural Development in Surul, carrying on the work that Elmhirst was doing, in teaching, working with the students to regenerate the village industries of weaving, carpentry, tannery, of gardening and agriculture and in participating in performing arts. Arthur also provided the link between Tagore and Geddes, in his father's absence, to take forward Geddes' plans and put them in place in relation to Tagore's ideals. His letters become a kind of diary of the development at Shantiniketan and Sriniketan during this period. It is during his stay that he not only learnt Bengali, but was able to sing and make notations for some of Tagore's songs, which he later compiled with the poet's prose translations, into a volume, after the poet's death. But what is also important, is Arthur's rendering of the songs on his violin, which permanently endeared this western instrument to Tagore, and his playing and singing of Scottish 'airs' to Tagore and his Bengali audience. The exchange was enriching on both sides and Tagore's exposition to Scottish tunes, which began much earlier in his famous adaptations of Robert Burns' songs in Bengali of 'Auld Lang Syne' as 'Purano shei diner katha' (1885) and of 'Ye Banks and Braes of Bonny Doon' as 'Phule phule, dhole dhole' (1882), mark the beginning of a lasting musical rapport between India and Scotland, as exemplified in Arthur Geddes' interest to introduce Tagore's melodies to the west, as the later letters show.

Charles Freer Andrews was, like, **W.W. Pearson**, a British missionary, both of whom had met Tagore in London in 1912. Both men visited Shantiniketan in 1913 and came to settle there in 1914.[19] At Shantiniketan, both are remembered affectionately, (Andrews more so for his longer association and hence more familiar figure) as 'Andrews saheb' and 'Pearson saheb' respectively. The 'saheb' has no connotation of colonial

---

[18] In 1895, Professor Zeublin of Chicago, was well justified in calling the Outlook Tower 'the world's first sociological laboratory... Its direct bearing upon education... was that it opened a way to the realm of learning by the most direct and familiar door, *i.e.*, by personal survey of the learner's own immediate environment. This had been Huxley's instinctive teaching method; and by Geddes it was developed into a comprehensive vision of life...' Philip Mairet, *Pioneer in Sociology: The Life and Letters of Patrick Geddes* (London: Lund Humphries, 1957) p. 72. What were once considered as side-lines were later incorporated in 'nature study' and geography.

[19] See Dutta and Robinson, 1995, p. 20.

deference, but the respect offered to two men who were undeniably 'sahebs', yet lost to Britain, having embraced and been appropriated by Anglo-India. Andrews was also responsible for introducing Tagore to Gandhi, the two giant figures of India in those days, who stood apart in their response to non-cooperation but each held the other in high regard, till the end. And it was to Andrews, who was torn between his loyalties to both especially when they disagreed on India's political stand to British rule, that both owed a cementing force. The acknowledgement was, of course, mutual, as Tagore named this ascetic leader of the nation the Mahatma, the great soul and Gandhi addressed Tagore (as Nehru too did[20]), as Gurudev.

Leonard Elmhirst was the British agricultural economist who put into practice and took forward Tagore's idea of rural reconstruction at Sriniketan. Sriniketan 'inspired the Elmhirsts'[21] (Leonard and his wife, Dorothy Straight) to found the Dartington Trust at Dartington Hall in England. The Elmhirsts contributed substantial financial support to Sriniketan.

Dorothy Whitney Straight was the American heiress whom Elmhirst married. Her Trust money was utilized for Sriniketan and later went into founding the Dartington Trust in Devon, which holds the Elmhirst archives.

William Archer was an art critic and Keeper Emeritus of the Indian Section of the Victoria and Albert Museum.

Professor P.C. Mahalanobis was an Indian economist and secretary to Tagore.

Ananda Coomeraswamy was an art critic of Sri Lankan and British parentage who wrote a favourable review of Tagore's paintings.

Young was probably Howard Young, an American scholar.

---

[20] In a letter written to Kripalani after Tagore's death, Nehru speaks of Tagore as 'Gurudeva', Kripalani, 1962, pp. 398-399.
[21] Dutta and Robinson, 1995, p. 13.

THE PROJECT

I was interested in the friendship between Geddes and Tagore, so I read the letters that are in the National Library of Scotland. But this was only one side of the correspondence, though there were some copies of letters from Geddes to Tagore in the collection. I spoke about this to my former Professor and Head of Department of English at Jadavpur University, Dr. Kitty Scouler Dutta, a Scot who had spent many years of her teaching life in India. Professor Dutta said she had seen the correspondence in India. An Indian colleague of hers had suggested that she edit these letters. She did not do it. She felt that 'a Bengali should do it'. And she looked pointedly at me and said, 'I think you are the right person, considering your links with Scotland and India'. That clinched the issue! I had to do this – draw the correspondence from both sides of the globe to tell the story of two educationists who shared similar ideals and were able to communicate – in spite of the fact that they belonged to two opposing groups, of the colonizer and the colonized. Growing up in India, inevitably entrenched in the Guru-shishya (teacher-disciple) tradition as it were – which Rabindranath Tagore drew upon (and Geddes too unconsciously adopted in the way he gathered many disciples in the course of this career, *e.g.* in Victor Branford and Lewis Mumford), I *had* to heed the word of my teacher.[22]

THE TWAIN[23]

What brought the two together in a long continued exchange of ideas? Boardman has pointed out a certain affinity between the two men. 'Tagore's intuitive method of developing his school was completely different from P.G.'s, yet there was a strong affinity between these two utterly different minds and personalities...'[24]

---

[22] It is interesting to note that in one letter Arthur asks his father to let him know of future projects so that he can be the true disciple, student and son, and in another to Tagore, he refers to himself as Tagore's 'Chela' from the West.

[23] Arthur Geddes throws light on this meeting of minds and an intimacy in 'Two Friends: Rabindranath Tagore and Patrick Geddes', in *Annual Journal of Architecture, Structure and Townplanning*, 1961.

[24] Philip Boardman, *The World of Patrick Geddes: Biologist, Town Planner, Re-educator, Peace Warrior* (London: Routledge, 1978), p. 333.

One can begin with the respect and impact they had while they lived. Both suited their respective roles as they looked their part: Patrick Geddes as the intellectual, untidy and totally un-selfconscious Professor and Rabindranath Tagore as Poet-Philosopher and Eastern Sage, which belied his very practical and rational approach to various national and international concerns and education.[25] In fact, Geddes was called 'the Professor' in his lifetime, while Tagore was referred to as 'the Poet'.

What made their thoughts so similar? Was it their respective backgrounds? Both men had a similar puritanical upbringing, in fact almost spartan, without the luxuries and embellishments of opulence or indulgence. Both were strongly influenced by their fathers. '[Geddes'] father – a retired soldier ... had a profound but benign effect on his life. Living in a modest cottage on the outskirts of Perth, Alexander Geddes had reared his youngest child in a way which unconsciously embodied most of the basic principles of what we now consider to be enlightened education.' Geddes too 'tried to rear his children in this way, so that love and care of plants and animals, the enjoyment of painting, singing and dancing, were as important as reading and numeracy. And everyone, he felt, should have practical experience of as many crafts as possible.'[26]

---

[25] Of Geddes' appearance, we have these two corroborating descriptions: 'Slight, untidy, always hurrying, with a shock of wiry hair parted in the middle and a thick, reddish beard, he was the traditional storybook professor. And he was invariably talking... a continuous, life-long monologue as he strove to inspire others with his vision of a combined knowledge, where the arts and sciences harmonized for the benefit of society... In short bursts his company was exhilarating, an elixir... (in the long run – exhausting!).' Kitchen, p. 18. And again, '... this man, regarded by some of the conventionally academic as little better than an interloper, looked more like a professor than any of them. He was rather of small stature; but with his leonine head-piece, crowned with a dark shock of hair parted in the middle, his eyes luminous with intelligence and geniality, and a beard worthy of a Greek Orthodox bishop, he looked the archetype of the man of learning. Edinburgh townsfolk naturally adopted the Scots habit of calling him simply 'The Professor', and so did many other people in non-academic circles when he became an international celebrity.' Mairet, *Pioneer of Sociology: The Life and Letters of Patrick Geddes*, Introduction, Arthur Geddes, (London: Lund Humphries, 1957) p. 61.

In a paper I presented at the School of Oriental and African Studies, I begin by saying, 'People who saw him [Tagore] at a performance in Oberammergau dressed in his long robes and turban, exclaimed "How like our Prophet!"' (Desai, 'Re-reading Tagore' in *Journal of Commonwealth Literature*, 29/1, 1994, p. 6). A member of the Tagore family told me that on the street of a European city, a father was walking with his child when they spotted Tagore. The father asked the child, 'Who do you think that is?' The child's unhesitating reply was 'Oh, that is God!' It is needless to add that the father did know who Tagore was. That was the impact Tagore had many times while he lived.' (*Tagore in and on Education: Retracing Journeys*, unpublished), p.1.

[26] Kitchen, 1975, p. 21

In spite of the lavish list of clothes items (and shoes) for 'Rabi' in the Tagore family cashbook,[27] Tagore's memory of his childhood and boyhood days echoes Geddes' own experience, 'Luxury was a thing almost unknown in my early childhood ... A list of our articles of clothings would only invite the modern boy's scorn'.[28] Maharshi Debendranath Tagore, Tagore's father, did not follow in the footsteps of his luxury-loving father, Dwarakanath, known as Prince Dwarakanath for his lavish style of entertaining and generous spending. In his spiritual autobiography, on the night of his grandmother's death on 21 December 1843, he writes of his epiphanic experience: sitting on the banks of the Ganges, he 'suddenly' felt 'a strange sense of the unreality of all things... A strong aversion to wealth arose within me. The coarse bamboo-mat on which I sat seemed to be my fitting seat, carpets and costly spreadings seemed hateful, in my mind was awakened a joy unfelt before.'[29] It is perhaps this streak of ascetic self-denial that Rabindranath Tagore's father inculcated in Tagore. Tagore concedes in 'My School', 'Fortunately for me I was brought up in a family where literature, music and art had become instinctive'.[30] The result of their upbringing reared a love of gardens and the open in both men, which they built into their respective educational institutions.

In questions of popular politics, they took the same kind of stand. Though Rabindranath Tagore led the Swadeshi Movement in protest against Lord Curzon's Divide and Rule policy in the first Partition of Bengal in 1905, he disassociated himself from politics when the wave of nationalism took to violence and remained a lone voice even in the face of Gandhian mass mobilisation for passive resistance. So, in effect, both Patrick Geddes and Rabindranath Tagore stood apart from politics. 'Conventional politics, ... were virtually irrelevant to his [Geddes'] life, since the whole structure of opposing parties was quite contrary to his beliefs in co-operation, and could not, ... lead to anything abidingly useful for the community... He utterly opposed violence for political ends...'[31] So they both remained emissaries of peace.

They had strong ideas on nationalism. 'Geddes' own Scottish patriotism was deep but not of the kind that flattered ordinary nationalistic

27 See Dutta and Robinson, p. 45.
28 Rabindranath Tagore, *Reminiscences* (Madras: Macmillan, 1917, rpt. 1971), pp. 8,9.
29 Dutta and Robinson, 1995, pp. 28-29.
30 Kabir, 1961, p. 399.
31 Kitchen, 1975, p. 22.

sentiments either in Scotland or elsewhere. Fundamentally, it was a respect and love for regional rootedness and loyalty, for the unity of the folk in their place; that was a cause he would defend anywhere at any cost. But existing political alignments and divisions seldom interested him much; and with him it was axiomatic that the higher life of the mind transcended all frontiers.'[32] Humayun Kabir describes Tagore's political convictions which were that of a humanist intellectual, one who believed that '...Love and respect for ideals of one's people is a positive virtue while disrespect for the ideals and traditions of others is a crime against humanity.' Tagore condemned in unqualified terms the aggressive nationalism which had raised the Nation State to a demi-god. He proclaimed that 'blind worship of the nation and the Nation State contained the seeds of disaster for man.'[33]

In the Foreword to Amelia Defries' book, Tagore says of Geddes 'he has the precision of the scientist and the vision of the prophet; and at the same time, the power of the artist to make his ideas visible through the language of symbols.'[34] The letters between Geddes and Tagore show that the respect was mutual.

Philip Boardman writes of a later attitude of Patrick Geddes: 'a sort of domineering impatience when confronted by the questions or objections raised by other mortals'.[35] Boardman says that this has been explained by his second son, Arthur, as 'a trait unconsciously acquired by his father by long years of association with essentially uncritical Indians. If, as it has been said, there were only three people in Britain capable of understanding and judging P.G., then there were none in India'[36] (a rather sweeping statement which has the danger of a kind of stereotyping that can develop to obfuscate the finer issues). I wish to take this up by first saying that Geddes spent nine 'long years' in India, metaphorically long when one appreciates the amount of work he did there in less than a decade of his very active 78 years. The charge of uncritical acceptance and/or adulation of Indians suggestive of these lines could perhaps be answered by the fact that there were, at least, two Indians who understood Geddes for what he was, a man

[32] Mairet, 1957, p. 62.
[33] Kabir 1961, p. 21.
[34] Amelia Defries, *The Interpreter Geddes: The Man and the Gospel, Introduction by Israel Zangwill* (London: George Routledge and Sons Ltd. 1927).
[35] Boardman, 1944, p. 397.
[36] Ibid.

far ahead of his times. They were Dr. Jagadish Chandra Bose, the biophysicist whose biography Geddes wrote (and the correspondence with him is in the National Library of Scotland to substantiate this meeting of minds), and Rabindranath Tagore – and it is their correspondences with which I would like to validate this point.

Tagore said of Geddes in his letter of 9 May 1922 that he was the kind of man who not only had 'a vast comprehensive sympathy and imagination, but also a wide range of knowledge and critical acumen'. And in Thomas Barclay's letter to Geddes in 1930, he says of Tagore, 'I am sure there is no more earnest votary for peace than a man who is one of the glories of the British Empire, and the moral link between Eastern and Western civilisations.'

People are beginning to see the 'need for his [Geddes'] vision and realism.'[37] And the same could be said of Tagore. There is now, a growing interest in the long and close association between Patrick Geddes and Rabindranath Tagore. However, earlier, as in Krishna Kripalani's biography *Rabindranath Tagore* (New York, Grove Press, 1962) there is only one mention of Tagore's association with Patrick Geddes when he says that in 1921 in Paris he 'made the acquaintance of Patrick Geddes whom he grew to admire' (p. 285). Later on in the book, when he cites the names of the international scholars who came to Shantiniketan where Tagore envisaged the meeting and exchange of intellects from East and West, Kripalani mentions 'Arthur Geddes from Scotland' (p.302). In *Rabindranath Tagore: The Myriad-Minded Man*, there is mention of Geddes, 'the Scot pioneer of town and regional planning,' who 'was in India for a while and offered his help to Tagore'[38] and again, in relation to an excerpt from one of his letters used in the earlier reference in relation to Tagore's own manner of working without plans and diagrams – unlike Geddes – but from an idea in his mind, for otherwise, he would not feel stimulated enough to continue (p. 330).

[37] See Mairet, 1957, p. 77.
[38] Dutta and Robinson, 1995, p. 10.

THE LETTERS

It has not been an easy task as deciphering the written hand can sometimes prove not just difficult, but impossible. Tagore's hand is clear, but Geddes' pen seems to trip over his ideas which come tumbling over the page, and are sometimes lost in words and lines crossed out, scribbled additions above already crowded lines and included in margins and sometimes irretrievable smudges, which blot out whole words in places. Then there are the famous Geddesian abbreviations like 'Santin.' or 'Edn.' or 'Envt.' with the last letter sometimes written above the actual word, to denote 'Santiniketan', 'Edinburgh' or 'environment', respectively. Some letters in the collections are typed copies or even photocopies with the right-hand corners of the original curled up, which has led to truncated last lines. I can remember one typed letter of Geddes in which the 't's start off as a top hat without the curved umbrella handle at the bottom and then disappear altogether in the course of the letter. This particular letter had the challenge of a crossword puzzle! Professor Swapan Majumdar, Acharya of Rabindra-Bhavana, suggested I include the letters of 'luminaries' who were part of the Geddes-Tagore circle. His advice has been invaluable, as apart from the letters by and to Geddes and Tagore, the ones from others in this group of not only Arthur Geddes, but from Andrews, Elmhirst, Pearson, Mahalanobis or Barclay, provide some of the missing links in the chain of correspondence. Some letters, of course, are not there, either at the Rabindra-Bhavana or in the National Library of Scotland collection. Some of the 'circle' could prove a problem. Andrews' writing appears a clear well spaced sprawl at a first glance, but can prove difficult to discern as letters slide into each other and blur. Some letters exist as typed copies of letters, of which the originals are not in either Rabindra-Bhavana or at the National Library of Scotland. Here I have accepted the interpretation of the original hand by the typist in full faith of it being honest, if not always, correct.

Apart from the difference in character of the written hand, the letters in themselves are very different. While Patrick Geddes' letters are usually long, descriptive, explaining his ideas in detail, Tagore's are short, but nevertheless, succinct. When the responses do appear, we see that Tagore does answer the points raised by Geddes in his letters, even if he may do so in one paragraph. Tagore wrote profusely, his ideas were captured not just in his creative pieces, but laid out in talks and essays and letters, which were all for publication and most often, *did* see print. Thus we find references to his ideas and thoughts in such essays as Geddes refers to in his letters to Tagore when he praises Tagore's ideas in 'Forest' or 'Education' or his satirical story 'The Parrot's Training'. Unlike Tagore's straight writing, Patrick Geddes made prodigious notes on paper (often folded two or three times[39] which became a habit with him after a threat of blindness[40]) with diagrams, sketches, lists, sub-headings, outlines and charts. But of all these ideas, which are a prodigious task for future scholars to put together and publish (and we hope they will, for the world to benefit from them), only a little of his sole authorship exists as complete publications *e.g.* in *Cities in Evolution, the Dunfermline Report, Talks from the Outlook Tower, Indore Report, Dramatizations of History* (co-published in India), and *An Indian Pioneer: the Life and Works of Sir J.C. Bose*. Apart from the last two, all these books are related to his town planning, architecture and landscape development theories and interests. But like Tagore, Geddes was an educationist and a socio-ecologist who believed in village reconstruction and land regeneration, which could be facilitated through the initiative of universities, and the latter in their turn, could be international in scope, and sensitive in their development. Tagore wrote again and again on his ideas about what education for Indians should be in essays such as 'The Vicissitudes of Education', 'The Problem of Education', 'Hindu University', 'The Centre of Indian Culture', 'The Unity of Education', 'A Poet's School', 'My School' and 'The Religion of the Forest'. Geddes' letters to Tagore, in their detailed discussion of his ideas, are a testimony to his ideas of what a full education should be. Hence the importance of this correspondence.

Geddes shares Tagore's ideals of universal education in harmony with life, effected in close bonds with nature, conscious as he was of man's environment. The ideas are their own, yet the resemblance is apparent – strong echoes in similar minds, but not mere imitations of each other. This similarity in thought and the desire to see their implementation in

---

[39] 'Geddes... invented a series of diagrams which he described as 'thinking machines': graphic methods for encouraging different ways of thinking. By using these thinking machines Geddes hoped to initiate and educate others to accept the need for educational reform and the need to pursue a synthesis of all knowledge.' (Helen Meller, *Patrick Geddes: Social Evolutionist and City Planner* (London and New York, Routledge, 1990) p. 45
[40] Preface by Israel Zangwill in Defries, 1927, p. 4.

educational institutions, is what brought them close to each other, and nurtured a life-long correspondence after they 'met'. I have intentionally put 'met' within inverted commas, as their exchange of letters could well have started months before they actually met, introduced to each other by mutual friends, through correspondence. Another reason why the letters are important is that their meetings were rare and far between, interrupted by their busy lives, their restless travels and intervening ill health. So the letters became the medium through which they both tried to express, develop and describe their ideas, ideals, their experiences and their work. Geddes' plans for an ideal university did not see full fruition in his lifetime, and this is why the letters are so important as they embody Geddes' and Tagore's ideas of an ideal international university. Such a university would bring people of every discipline from across the world, together in an intellectual exchange,[41] where the teacher and student would both be residents in an intimate atmosphere of learning, from where they would reach out to adjoining rural areas and communities, extending their knowledge in an ever-expanding compass, to enrich and develop the surroundings in a mutual bond of harmony.

The letters are important today, when war seems to be, not a nightmare of the past, but raging in various parts of the world and a constant

---

[41] Of Geddes' Summer Meetings, Boardman writes, 'Each August for a dozen years the Lawnmarket quarter of Edinburgh became the focus towards which men of fresh ideas converged from the British Isles, Continental Europe, and America. Amongst them at different times were well-known men like Emile Yung, Swiss botanist; Ernst Haeckel, the great German evolutionist, and Henri de Varigny, French biologist: also from France came Paul Desjardins, publicist and philosopher; Abbé Felix Klein, educator; Edmond Desmolins, the continuator of Le Play; Elisée Reclus, renowned geographer, and his brother Elie the anthropologist. From Scotland, England and Ireland came an equal number of prominent teachers, scientists and men of letters, while America contributed William James of Harvard, Charles Zeubin of Chicago and many others.' In Mairet, 1957, p. 64. Of the summer school Boardman also says, 'it is the story of high intellectual adventure along the road that leads towards unity of knowledge and culture.' Ibid. p. 157.
Similarly, 'Tagore's dream of making Shantiniketan a nest where kindred spirits would gather from different parts of the world was coming true. What was originally planned as a hermitage was becoming a cosmopolitan beehive. Besides the three remarkable Englishmen, Andrews, Pearson and Elmhirst, there was the French savant Sylvain Levi and his wife, ...the no less eminent Orientalist Moritz Winternitz of the German University in Prague and later by Professor V. Lesny of the Charles University. Among other distinguished visiting scholars ... [were] Stella Kramrisch, art historian and critic (later of University of Pennsylvania), F. Benoit, a French-Swiss linguist, L. Bogdanov, a Russian scholar of Persian and Pehlevi, Arthur Geddes from Scotland, Stanley Jones and Miss Gretchen Green from the United States, and Miss S. Flaum, a Jewish lady who graduated from the University of Columbia.' Kripalani, 1962, p. 302. To these names one might add others like the two Italian scholars, Formichi and Tucci and the famous Japanese poet, Yone Noguchi.

threat to all nations, from without and within. Both Geddes and Tagore believed in the probability and necessity of a union between East and West through intellectual understanding, developing into mutual respect, which could be effected by the leadership given by International Universities working together, in what Geddes foresaw as the 'League of Academic Nations' or what we would probably call today the organization of 'United Academic Nations'.

While Geddes was interested in the planning of Tagore's Visva-Bharati, with Arthur's help as an on-the-spot emissary and representative (though, as stated earlier, circumstances prevented the proper implementation of these plans), Tagore, on Geddes' invitation, became the President of the Indian College at Montpellier, which Geddes established alongside the Scots College there.

To standardise the text of the correspondence, some decisions have been taken. The dates when the letters were written have been given a similar pattern. The signature with the final formalities is centred. All abbreviations have been spelt out. Where one is ninety percent sure of having read the word correctly, but there is room for a little doubt, the word is italicised; but where it is totally indecipherable, it is explained as '[illegible]'. The letters have been arranged in chronological order to make them easy to find in the book.

The letters from Gandhi to Young and from Tagore to Young put all three men in perspective, showing the links between them and the public concerns of the times. Moreover, Geddes had a brief but warm relationship with Gandhi during his initial years in India.

From the letters we can see that in 1914 Tagore's school at Shantiniketan is in full swing (having been inaugurated on 21 December 1901,[42]) as the ideas of his *Ashram* show in his reference to it in a letter to Young at this time. So we know that Tagore thinks of his institution as one in line with the *tapovana*,[43] the hermitages or forest refuges of ancient

---

[42] Dutta and Robinson, 1995, p. 135.

[43] 'Our tapovanas, which were our natural universities, were not isolated from life. There the masters and students lived their full life; they gathered fruit and fuel; they took their cattle to graze; and the spiritual education, which the students had, was a part of the spiritual life itself which comprehended all life. Our centre of culture should not only be the centre of the intellectual life of India, but the centre of her economic life as well.' 'The Centre of Indian Culture', in Kabir, 1961, p. 227.

[continued overleaf]

India. Pearson is mentioned and so is Andrews with humour, showing their intimacy with the poet. Both played important roles in the life and shaping of Tagore's school and university.

On 16 December 1914 William Archer writes a letter of introduction for Professor Patrick Geddes as a well-known biologist and sociologist to Andrews and hopes he will ensure that Geddes sees the 'right things and people in India'. This is on the eve of Geddes' departure to India, where he came for the first time in October 1914.[44] He had a long relationship with India till he had to leave on health grounds in 1923, after which he settled in the south of France and worked on the Scots College and the Indian College. Andrews' friendships with Tagore and Gandhi are well known. He was obviously instrumental in bringing Geddes close to both these intellectuals he regarded and loved, as the letters between Andrews, Patrick and Arthur Geddes and Tagore, indicate, even if we cannot be sure as to whether he actually introduced them to each other or not.

So, when did the twain first meet? In Krishna Kripalani's biography,[45] there is only one mention of Tagore's association with Patrick Geddes when he says that in 1921 in Paris he 'made the acquaintance of Patrick Geddes whom he grew to admire' (p. 285). One may wonder if this was, indeed, the first face-to-face meeting of the 'two great souls'. In April 1922 Geddes refers in a letter to Tagore of their meeting in Paris 'last summer' which would tally with Kripalani's statement. Yet in 1920, when Tagore writes his foreword for Defries' book, he speaks about coming to know Geddes in

'... The gurus of ancient India, so tradition says, lived in hermitages... the guru was a family man and his pupils lived with him as members of his household. The idea that the teacher and his pupils should live together has come down to the present day and is sometimes found in our *tols* and *chatuspathis*, schools and colleges that provide orthodox Hindu learning...' 'The Problem of Education', ibid., p. 70.

One encounters a similar response in Geddes and his deep understanding of Indian culture when he writes, of India '... It rests on sacred and epic literature and legend for the people, and on great and ancient philosophies, which are not merely cultivated by the classically educated, but deeply diffused, for good and evil, throughout the people as well. All this variety of cultural influences, in essential harmony and... free from intolerance, has from unnumbered ages been steeping into the Indian villages with their old economic self-sufficiency and moral solidarity...' Patrick Geddes, *An Indian Pioneer: the Life and Work of Sir J.C. Bose* (New Delhi and Madras: Asia Educational services, 2000) p. 116, p. 324.

[44] In a letter to his wife addressed 'Dear Folk' Geddes writes against an entry of 23 October 'busy day' at Poona and ends with news of the German raider, Emden's sinking of 'Clan Grant', the freighter with his entire 'Cities Exhibition'. He ends saying with some characteristic 'bravado' as Philip Mairet puts it, 'Are we downhearted? NO!' Mairet, 1957, p. 156.

[45] Kripalani, 1962, p. 285.

India, which could mean, forming a greater understanding of the person, and his ideals through his approach and work. This, one could surmise, was from reports of Geddes' work in India and not necessarily from personal encounters or witnessing Geddes at work. But Philip Boardman writes under his sub-heading THE POET'S UNIVERSITY AT SANTINIKETAN:

> Unlike the brief encounter with Gandhi, Geddes achieved a lasting friendship and co-operation with the poet Rabindranath Tagore, dating from the Darjeeling Summer Meeting in 1917. Their closest contact, however, was in 1922-23 and concerned the latter's plans for an 'International University in India'.
>
> P.G. outlined ... a coordination of arts and sciences which he claimed would satisfy both conventional academics and poets. Though he progressed from logic, with which 'the traditional University began', through mathematics and natural sciences to those of men and society, Geddes did not box them into thinking machines. Instead, he used 'Conduct', 'Behaviour' and 'Activity' as three simple terms which revealed without 'academic jargon, the world-old simplicity, since unity, of Life'; and even explained them in linear prose, partly aided by arrows and parenthesis...[46]

The letters exchanged in June 1918 indicate that Geddes has already established a correspondence and rapport with Tagore. The reference is to Tagore's delightfully told satire on the predicament of a parrot in the story 'The Parrot's Training' (the memorable 'Tota Kahini' in Bengali). The parrot becomes the target of bureaucratic training and experiment and is forgotten of and dies in the process. We find Geddes agreeing with Tagore's ideas on ideal education, refuting the rote method and the unnecessary fanfare that goes before actual education can start; where the student is the least considered object and where humanity is missing. The rebel in both Geddes and Tagore to existing faulty education systems is apparent at this early stage of their acquaintance.[47] Tagore's school has been visited by Dr.

---

[46] Boardman, 1978, pp. 331, 332. Boardman continues to explain that the purpose of such a University 'was to pave "the path to a future when both the East and West will work together for the general cause of human welfare."' Ibid., p. 331.

[47] Geddes and Tagore shared a suspicion of the examination system and did not take any degrees. 'Geddes had a deep disdain for all academic drudgery, and he adamantly refused to take degree examinations'. Dutta and Robinson speak of 'Tagore's [continued overleaf]

Sadhu of Calcutta University, who has read the story and agrees on 'all vital things about education' as Tagore says. Here is the first mention of the need for 'an ideal university in some of our Native States' by Tagore, and he raises the question of instruction in a native tongue at a new university, as suggested by the Nizam State, seeking Geddes' opinion on this matter. Tagore's life-long struggle was to establish the mother tongue as the medium of instruction at Indian institutions, not just at his own Shantiniketan. Geddes, in full agreement with Tagore's view, deplores the end to such dreams by the unimaginative 'Translation Bureau' of 'bad textbooks' that has been set up at Hyderabad University, in lieu of introducing Urdu with Professor Abdul Majid. He feels that only after the 'founding of free Institutes and Libraries and Outlooks of Initiation' (probably having his own Outlook Tower in mind), could 'Free and Reconstructive Universities' follow and flourish.

In 1919 Geddes praises Tagore on his essays on 'Education' and 'Forest' and hopes that he will 'erupt again over Calcutta University'. For Tagore, Calcutta University was prototypical of institutions which promulgated Western learning which had no relation to the reality of life in India, beginning with teaching in a foreign language. Geddes' interest in the lesson to be learnt from 'Parrot's Training' continued in his request for more copies of it and his circulation of it amongst many of his friends and colleagues. The lectures he refers to in his letter of 1919 are probably 'The Centre of Indian Culture' in which Tagore publicly set forth his ideas of an International University in India (delivered in Madras in 1919 and published by the Society for Promotion of National Education, Adyar, Madras) and 'The Religion of the Forest'.

In his essay 'The Centre of Indian Culture' Tagore says, 'In education the most important factor is an atmosphere of creative activity, in which the work of intellectual exploration may find full scope. The teaching should be like the overflow water of a spring of culture, spontaneous and

---

abhorrence of almost all formal education in India – including his own in Calcutta in the 1860s and 70s (he never matriculated, let alone took a university degree)...' Geddes was outspoken in his criticism of Edinburgh University, because of which, he failed to get the much-desired chair. So the part-time Professor's chair in Dundee, came as the recognition and scope for the expansion needed by Geddes for his own ideas. Tagore's 'attitude to academe would be a mixed one throughout his life... His relationship with Calcutta University was at best uneasy...' The university, however, did relent through Lord Hardinge's (the then viceroy of India) staunch overruling of all opposition, and confer an honorary degree on him, before the Nobel Prize, in October 1913. See Dutta and Robinson, 1995, pp. 59, 183.

inevitable. Education becomes natural and wholesome only when it is the fruit of a living and growing knowledge.

Further, our education should be in constant touch with our complete life, economic, intellectual, aesthetic, social and spiritual; and our schools should be at the very heart of our society, connected with it by the living bonds of varied co-operation. For, true education is to realize at every step how our training and knowledge have an organic connection with our surroundings.' (pp. 202-03).

He goes on to say how the thought of a university brings Oxford, Cambridge and other European ones to mind and how we think that the best points of each could 'patch together an eclectic perfection. We forget that European universities are organic parts of the life of Europe' (p. 204-05).

He says how we deplore lack of funds to establish buildings and buy furniture for our own institutions. Tagore goes on to say, 'We in the east have had to arrive at our own solution of the problems of life. We have, as far as possible, made our food and clothing unburdensome; our climate has taught us to do so. We require the openings in wall more than the walls themselves... I do not seek to glorify poverty. But simplicity is of greater value than the appendages of luxury' (Ibid., p. 206). Here, he echoes Geddes' own convictions of finding the solution to a problem by considering its context, of retaining as much as possible of what was existent and altering it to suit the needs of the place and people it would benefit, at minimum cost.

As Tagore was to prove through his efforts at Visva-Bharati, there is a need for the inspired (and inspiring) and dedicated teacher: 'To our misfortune we have in our country all the furniture of the European university – except the living teacher. We have instead purveyors of book-lore in whom the paper god of the bookshop seems to have made himself vocal.' (p. 209) He asks pertinent questions like 'Has it (European culture) any natural centre in India? Has it any vital, everflowing connection with her life?... none, [nor]... can have any; for the perennial centre of Europe is sure to be in Europe'. (p. 221) He gives the example of an Allahabad schoolboy who lived at the confluence of the rivers Ganges and Jamuna and gave an accurate description of a river when asked for one, but when he was asked whether he had seen any rivers, he said no! He did not know that the Ganges and the Jamuna were great rivers too! This is what Tagore means by saying that education should be a continuity of life's immediate experience, taking stock of one's surroundings and deriving knowledge from them. Geddes in his Outlook Tower, 'the world's first sociological laboratory' (1885-1914 under his immediate supervision), put into practise 'Huxley's instinctive teaching' method of 'personal survey of the learner's own immediate environment,' taking it further to embrace a detailed picture of all the continents and the universe. See *Philip Mairet, Pioneer of Sociology, The Life and Letters of Patrick Geddes*, (London, Lund Humphries, 1957, p. 72).

We see this same note of universality when Tagore goes on to say that 'the inner spirit of India is calling' for centres in the tradition of educational institutions (he does not want to call them universities for fear of inviting imitations of unsuitable models) like Taxila, Mithila and Nalanda and the forest retreats of Vedic times (of which he talks at length in 'The Religion of the Forest'). In such places 'intellectual forces will gather for the purpose of creation, and all resources of knowledge and thought, Eastern and Western, will unite in perfect harmony' (pp. 221-2). They were to be inclusive, providing 'co-ordinated study of... different cultures – the Vedic, the Puranic, the Buddhist, the Jain, the Islamic, the Sikh, and the Zoroastrian. And side by side with them the European – for then only shall we be able to assimilate it.' (p. 224) He is talking against the imposition of European culture from above, rather than its assimilation from within – a culture he knows and asserts as desirable. English should come in the course of an Indian student's studies, but not as an imposition and as the medium of instruction.[48] In a later essay he tells of the story of how the teaching of English was requested by his boys at Shantiniketan when they were posting some letters at the post office and witnessed their addresses, written in Bengali, being rewritten in English by the postmaster. They then came back to the teacher and asked for an extra hour of English. 'The boys never regretted their rash request.' ('A Poet's School', first published in 1926).[49]

---

[48] Tagore's argument sounds like Plato's where the artist in imitating an object of the real world, is twice removed from the truth of the idea. So is the Indian schoolboy, who must learn a language that is not his, and then of the world through that language, a world that has no reference to his own. And then he must try to match these pictures, once he has translated them to his familiar world – to which, of course, they do not match.

[49] Krishna Dutta and Andrew Robinson, ed. *Rabindranath Tagore, An Anthology* (Picador: London, 1997) p. 258.

In 'The Religion of the Forest' Tagore says how greed leads to multiplicity of external possessions. He speaks of the 'ideal of perfection preached by the forest-dwellers of ancient India' (p. 511) which runs through Indian classical literature, in which 'The hermitage shines out... as the place where the chasm between man and the rest of creation has been bridged' (p. 512). Kalidas' poetic compositions 'contain the voice of warnings against the gorgeous unreality of that age, which like a Himalayan avalanche, was slowly gliding down to an abyss of catastrophe.' (p. 514) His voyage through the Red Sea made him think of the two diverse civilizations on either side, of Egypt 'whose guardian-spirit is a noble river' which has fostered civilization 'rich with sentiments and expressions of life'.[50] On the other side there is Arabia beyond Aden, where 'man felt himself isolated in his hostile and bare surroundings'. The two civilizations, to Tagore, symbolize two fundamental divisions of human nature: the spirit of harmony and the spirit of conquest, both of which 'have their truth and purpose in human existence.' Given such choices, India has to remember that she 'holds sacred, and counts as places of pilgrimage, all spots which display a special beauty or splendour of nature... Here, man is free, not to look upon Nature as a source of supply of his necessities, but to realize his souls beyond himself.'[51] What Tagore is advocating is the centre of learning in an atmosphere of secluded openness, where teacher and students live together in simplicity and close to nature and education is tied with life's creative tasks, as in the *tapovana* ('forest hermitages or ashrams in ancient India where learned sages lived with their disciples and taught them the

---

[50] It is amazing that Geddes, in the same Sea, doing the reverse journey, coming from Europe to India, had similar thoughts, which he noted, of Egypt and Arabia, 'Nowhere else is such a perfect contrast to be seen, so far as my geography goes, as between this unresisting process of collapse into the sea on the one side, and the sublime resistance of these Arabian mountains on the other; with their nobly individualised sierra- and peak-alteration, keen against the sky. It was indeed interesting to recall this as the Sinaitic peninsula – with its great associations of the individuality, and Union, of God and Man.' And he continues in the same vein, '... I remembered we were beside the Peninsula of Sinai, and between this and the mountains of old Egypt; home of idealism each in its own way – but the spiritual and ethopolitic vision of the one far exceeding and transcending the geotechnic mastery of the other'. Boardman, Routledge, 1978, pp. 250, 251.

[51] Coming to Benares in early December in 1914, Geddes writes of 'this wonderful old city of religion' and goes on to analyse how religions 'hold back the cosmic stream, and make it the human one it is. Yet how simply! – that nature is sacred, that sex is sacred, that creatures are sacred, life sacred, and that even out of destruction comes new life; – these seem to be the main teachings; ...in a world where ideals, and meditations on them, are recognised as the main business of life...' Boardman, 1978, p. 255.

practice of simple living and high thinking.')[52] This practice echoes the old apprenticeship model of Europe, when the apprentice lived with his teacher as a household member and learnt the craft.

As referred to earlier, Tagore was asked to write a foreword in 1920 for Defries' book on Geddes. He writes about the deep impression Geddes made on him: 'the fullness of his personality' rose 'far above his science' because of 'his humanity'. Geddes personified what Tagore valued in the life-fashioning guru. It is befitting to give the foreword in full at this stage:

> What so strongly attracted me in Dr. Patrick Geddes when I came to know him in India was not his scientific achievements, but, on the contrary, the rare fact of the fullness of his personality rising far above his science. Whatever he has studied and mastered has become vitally one with his humanity. He has the precision of the scientist and the vision of the prophet, at the same time, the power of an artist to make his ideas visible through the language of symbols. His love of Man has given him the insight to see the truth of Man, and his imagination to realise in the world the infinite mystery of life and not merely its mechanical aspect.'[53]

Geddes' humanity matched with his scientist's precision and prophet's vision made him the right person for Tagore to share his scheme of an 'International University in India with the object of paving the path for a future when both the East and West will work together for the general cause of human welfare.' He makes this intention clearer to Geddes in 1921 when he sends him a copy of his Letter of Invitation for Geddes' advice and suggestions. We can see the same line of thought in Tagore in his wish to hold an Exhibition on Indian life and culture to encapsulate his lessons from past history and indicate his visions for future developments, which is very much in tune with Geddes' own method of telling whole histories in visual displays of this kind. We know how important Geddes' work is in relation to the building of the Outlook Tower and the Cities and Town Planning Exhibition, which, as mentioned earlier, he lost in a sea disaster. He succeeded in having it put together again from scratch for display at an exhibition in Madras which opened on 17 January, 1915.

[52] Kripalani, 1962, p. 189.
[53] Defries, 1957.

In a long letter to Tagore in 1922 Geddes draws the parallels between Tagore's work at Shantiniketan with his, the 'kindred beginnings' at the Outlook Tower through to Bombay, where the idea of Cities and Town Planning Exhibition shows the fruits of studying the surrounding regions (and cities). His inter-disciplinary approach, combining the scientific and technical approaches to the arts, of the bio-sciences to psychology and education, of economics and politics with ethics, bring about the novel combination of subjects for the future, of Eutechnics, Psychoorganics and Etho-polity/tics. This harmonised approach would replace the segmented Faculties that exist in conventional universities. He goes on to link his diagrammatic proposal about Life in conjunction with 'Conduct', 'Behaviour' and 'Activity', keeping in mind the application to life of interacting multi-faceted disciplines.

Tagore's response is typical of a creative artist to the scientist, who does not begin with a plan, but starts, as in his stories, with an 'emotional motive', with no 'definite outline'. His work at Shantiniketan, 'has been from first to last a growth', as he says. The rebel in him refuses to be bound by a scheme of things, for he needs the constant 'stimulation of surprises'. However, he confesses that he too has grown with the Institution, as it has been 'an incessant lesson' to him. His first task was to emancipate his students' minds from all barriers. There is the hint that this is just a beginning, as Shantiniketan expresses the conflicts of the 'present age', and becomes a creative force to express the changes. And then there is the ideal of an international institute, working towards the 'spiritual unity of human races' – not just an Indian endeavour for Indians only – as Geddes advocated in his Edinburgh Summer School from 1887 till 1900 (except for one revival in 1903, Mairet, 1957, p. 67) and at the Scots and Indian College at Montpellier from 1923, both of which were very international in outlook. He acknowledges his 'bewilderment of admiration' for a person like Geddes for 'the architectural immensity of his vision' and says he has been looking for men like him for his own 'mission'. The ambivalence in Tagore's answer is typical of the artist's response to the scientist's approach. There is the acknowledged admiration for the man – his training, his perspectives and his vision, but a certain caution as to his scheme of things, a stubborn reluctance to conform to diagrams and formulated plans. The ambivalence continues, as he assures him in the end that he will file Geddes' ideas away in his mind, for 'living assimilation' just like the assimilation he envisages of European culture in his own university! But he does detect that Geddes' schemes 'have the same element' as his ideal but expressed in 'a different idiom'.

Geddes' answer concedes the dryness of all technical plans because of their mathematical nature, but he, like Tagore, wishes for universities to achieve 'spiritual and ideal' completeness. In this letter, he gives the intersecting triangles which he designed for the Great Hall at Jerusalem University,[54] to symbolize the great Jewish tradition of unity, a graphic illustration of his idea of Synthesis.[55] Here he echoes an idea of Tagore's, of the necessity of the Environment working on Organism, but the Organism ultimately masters the Environment. In this letter, he also formulates his famous idea of the inter-relation that needs to exist between Place, People (Folk as he says elsewhere) and Work. Arthur picks up this idea of his father's when he works on planning the University during his teaching period of Sriniketan at Surul, the sister institution of Shantiniketan, that Elmhirst supervised and saw grow. Arthur developed Elmhirst's work in his absence when he was at Sriniketan from March 1923. Here Geddes, with an impish sense of humour and understanding, uses a metaphor appealing to a poet, philosopher and composer, drawing on the inherent harmony in such a scheme for both the 'philosophic harp' and the 'poet's lyre', drawing on the analogy of notations: he for his thoughts and the poet for his songs.

Geddes spends two crowded active days at Surul with Arthur in the beginning of November 1922, in the poet's absence, surveying the place, noting in detail the geography, the layout of the institutions (Shantiniketan and Sriniketan), the anomalies in the development and the scope for construction and reconstruction.[56] His questions show his deep interest and

---

[54] Geddes went to formulate plans there for an International University on the invitation of the Zionist Federation in 1919. Of all his plans, only his one of the Library found fruition.
[55] The 'Hebrew University of Jerusalem on Mount Scopus [is on] the 'Hill of Vision'... It is a superb design for a university, hexagonal in plan, with the faculties of arts, sciences, and technology radiating from a great domed assembly hall in the centre. Studied in the light of the accompanying report, the design is itself a liberal education in the religion between the different cultural functions. Hebraic studies are accommodated in one large wing, a sort of peninsula jutting out to the south-west, its isthmus occupied by the history of languages.' ...'the dome is of universal use for religious expression... that which expresses, on the small human scale, the great dome of the heavens.' Mairet, 1957, pp. 185, 187.
[56] Boardman speaks of Geddes' methods which included his 'insistence on "diagnosis before treatment"' and 'his practice of "conservative surgery"'... 'P. G. would ridicule the plan with an effective combination of seriousness and sarcasm, and then make a better and cheaper one' From the *Indore Report*, in Boardman, 1978, p. 283.

the wide scope of his vision, from the present and expected number of students to the intended subjects and their range. Like Tagore, he wanted to see that there was room for the old and the new – in Indian and European languages, both classical and modern. In this letter he sees the parallels in his Summer School at Shantiniketan and of his vision to Tagore's, though he concedes that Tagore aims for all-the-year-round work.

Nonetheless, Geddes feels that Tagore cannot compete right now with established institutions like Oxford, Cambridge, Harvard and Chicago – an analogy Tagore had wanted to avoid as he makes clear in essays such as 'The Centre of Indian Culture'.[57] He goes on to say that what they were planning for Jerusalem University would surpass the great names, which, given the chance, he is sure, all these institutions will robustly protest! His advice is that Tagore should concentrate on Agriculture, Fine Arts, Music, Ancient and Modern Literature and leave other institutions to run Law, Medical and Engineering Faculties. This is exactly what Tagore did, but he did introduce the conventional Science and Humanities faculties and added Chinese, Japanese and Tibetan studies to Visva-Bharati, to bring the immediate East and the Far East to the concept of all-embracing harmony which Tagore envisaged for a modern institution.

Tagore meets Geddes in Bombay once but the long talk they have agreed on does not take place as Tagore leaves Bombay, which causes some hurt. Here we find the two share a trait of acute sensitivity to hurt, for time and time again Tagore is upset by the misinterpretation of his message or bad and even hostile reception to and publicity of his stand and his creative work. Andrews testifies to Geddes' 'very sensitive' nature, 'like all Celts'. Through his correspondence Geddes acts as a mediator in trying to bring two well-known Bengalis to work together as he implies how both Tagore and the famous bio-physicist Dr. J.C. Bose are similar in fighting 'battles' for their causes. Andrews conveys Geddes' wish that Tagore establish a fellowship with Bose, allowing his student, Basiswar Sen to come and advise him 'on the science side'. Andrews sends the diagram of the plan for new residential quarters that he has worked out with Geddes and Arthur.

In this letter and in later ones, we find Geddes' inclination to work with the environment by his ongoing concern for the upkeep and maintenance of the Tank (a lake at Shantiniketan). His aversion for the

---

57 See Kabir, 1961, pp. 202-230.

complete demolition of an ugly wall by 'part revising and part building'[58] it comes across, and he gives the sound advice of investing in a good architect. Geddes also introduces the Parsee, Khambatta, who will be of help in acting and drama work and in planning the open theatre. Later, in a letter from Arthur to his father, we find a full description of a performance 'Masque of the Desert', which was not just to give Khambatta something to do, as Arthur writes to his father, but also to show how Khambatta combined the role and place of the performing arts at Shantiniketan and Sriniketan. The 'Surul boys' cut the channel to bring in water and the spirit of life, to push back the desert – symbolising the message of active work in close alliance with the environment to make education a continuation of life. We find the same desire for creative participatory activities in Geddes' summer schools.[59] However, 'Their close application to difficult studies was relieved by organized ones that doubtless included some high-spirited larking. And there were some activities which the school thought rightly important, such as its dramatic representations.' (This 'high-spirited larking', Mairet thinks, was, perhaps, one of the reasons as to why the municipal authorities withdrew their funds – just as abruptly as they had given them – thinking that they were, amongst other things, 'highly improper'[60]).

---

[58] 'He felt … that the diagnostic approach to the whole problem must include the physico-mental diagnosis of persons in community. For social and economic rehabilitation, the sick *Folk*, falteringly at *work* in ruined *Places*, must renew their own latent power of goodwill. This alone, guided by survey and by synthesis, could energize a Community for co-operation, for *Synergy*, towards new *Achievement*.' Here is the famous basis for his triad around the inter-related trio of People, Place and Work. Introduction, Arthur Geddes in Mairet, 1957, pp. xvii-viii.

[59] For Geddes' Summer School, see footnote 41. Geddes' letters to Tagore from Montpellier, especially from 1927, show similar ideas of education in close association with practical purposes in life being implemented and/or envisioned.

One can compare the activities at Shantiniketan with those at Geddes' Summer School. In 'A Poet's School' Tagore writes 'With the help of literature, festive ceremonials and religious teachings I tried to develop in the children of my school their feeling for Nature as also a sensitiveness to their human surroundings... Among the subjects they learnt in the open air, in the shade of trees, were music and painting, and they had their dramatic performances. But this was not sufficient, and I waited for men and the means to be able to introduce into our school activities that build up character. I felt the need of the western strength of reality which knew how to achieve a definite end of practical good... [This is where the assistance of Geddes, his son Arthur and that of Elmhirst came in useful to fill the gap Tagore perceived in his institution.] They take great pleasure in cooking, weaving, gardening, improving their surroundings, and in rendering services to other boys, very often secretly, lest they should feel embarrassed.' Dutta and Robinson, 1997, pp. 296, 298.

[60] Mairet, 1957, pp. 66, 67.

38

Tagore's gratitude and admiration for Geddes' plans need to be stressed here in spite of the note of impatience and lack of faith in Geddes' letter of 26 February 1923, to Mahalanobis, Secretary to Tagore. He is obviously relying on Arthur's 'efficient guidance' to make a place for Geddes' proposal in his institution, to translate Geddes' graphic representation of the growth of human life and mind.

A link in the chain is lost as Tagore confesses that he has lost Geddes' letter in the turmoil of the Governor of Bengal's visit to the 'Ashram'. The Governor's visit shows an official recognition of his Institution, and the 'Ashram' endorses Tagore's renewal of the ancient Indian *tapovana* in a modern context. We see how Tagore is caught up with raising funds for the Bengal floods as is Andrews. Later, in a letter from Elmhirst to Geddes we learn how Andrews will be totally unavailable because of these floods, absorbed as he is in relief work, and we also get Elmhirst's estimation of Andrews as well meaning and good hearted but as one who does not fully grasp the poet's ideals. And it is on such people that Geddes will depend, while Tagore is busy writing or putting on performances, lecturing, giving talks elsewhere, all to raise funds for his institute whose growth was always interrupted by the lack of dependable funds. Later on, with Dorothy Whitney's Trust money which she gave over to her husband Elmhirst, to use as he pleased at Sriniketan, this part of the institution saw a steady realization of Tagore's ideals in rural reconstruction. Elmhirst also corroborates the 'impossible' delays to Geddes' plan and accounts for it as the inevitable result of having to depend on inefficient labour. In this letter there are references to photographs he is taking and an expensive film he is making, the first for Geddes, and the second to raise money for the work at Surul. The film is never mentioned again in the whole course of the Geddes-Tagore correspondence. One wonders if the photographs that the architect Vowan Rao sent to Geddes as Arthur mentions in a letter to his father in March 1923, were the same ones that Elmhirst took.

Mahalanobis' (secretary at Shantiniketan) letter assures Geddes, early in 1923, that Rathi is 'actively preparing Geddes' plan'. He also proposes that he will, at the next Governing Body Meeting of Visva-Bharati, obtain the official sanction for making Geddes Tagore's representative in America. The problem of money is a sad ghost that hovers over Visva-Bharati all through the years till 1940, when an ailing and tired Tagore, in a hand-written note to Gandhi on what was to be the latter's last visit to the

Ashram, asks the Mahatma to take 'this institution under your protection, giving it an assurance of permanence if you consider it to be a national asset'.[61] And Gandhi did. In his reply he said, 'Gurudev himself is international, and he is truly national. Therefore, all his creation is international, and Visva-Bharati is the best of all'.[62] It is today one of India's national universities and still attracts a few international scholars, though staffed by Indians, but it does not really mirror Tagore's ideal of seeing the interplay of thought between itinerant gurus from both the East and the West, meeting and staying there for short periods.[63]

The lack of a stable fund and the subsequent strain of fund-raising interrupted the formulation of a step by step plan for Tagore's university which Geddes so wanted to lend his assistance and expertise for. We find Tagore in agreement with Geddes about utilising Khambatta's services and his worries about raising enough money to have a chair for Dr. Brajendranath Seal at his university.

Geddes' letter to Mahalanobis on the eve of his departure to America in February 1923 shows the Celtic hurt that Andrews' letter to Tagore refers to earlier. The plans have come, but too late. Geddes is on the point of departure. Other institutions have requested his help and their Principals at Osmania and Ahmedabad have worked on the ground with him. Tagore has left Bombay without the promised 'business talk' (although he concedes that he did come to see the Exhibition); the seeming neglect understandably rankles. In this letter is the hint of having listened to criticism about Tagore and his work 'from others less friendly than I', which might have influenced his judgement momentarily about Tagore and his institution. Tagore now stood apart in the Indian political scene as a non-conformer to the spinning of the charka[64] and in declining to support the Non-cooperation Movement which he saw as one that would lead to a different kind of violence, which Gandhi did not foresee.[65] Geddes, however, does

---

[61] Kripalani, 1962, p. 388.
[62] Ibid.
[63] The system of 'exchanging' Professors of different universities for short periods, as in America, should be adopted. Rabindranath Tagore, 'Universities' in *The Modern Review*, April 1919, vol xxv, no. 1, p. 389.
[64] Of the charka, Tagore said to Gandhi, 'Poems I can spin, Gandhiji, songs and plays I can spin, but of your precious cotton what a mess I would make!' Dutta and Robinson, 1995, p. 240.
[65] See Tagore's essay 'The Call of Truth' and Gandhi's answer in an essay whose title became a shrewd summing up of Tagore, *i.e.*, 'The Great Sentinel'.

say in the same letter that he will communicate on further development of plans with Arthur at Surul. Geddes was touchy, like his friend Tagore, who, many a time, when facing criticism, even cancelled his lectures and abandoned his tours abroad. To be fair to Geddes' broad vision, when his ship, the *Adriatic* reached New York on May 7, he told reporters there 'about Tagore's newly-created university at Shantiniketan in Bengal, and about his own part in helping the poet plan it'.[66]

The wound in the relationship heals soon. In the letters between Arthur and his father during the former's stay at Shantiniketan in 1923, of Andrews to Geddes and Geddes to Tagore, we see how Geddes' memory retains every detail, as he goes over with Arthur the plans for the Tank, the Temple, the possibility of an open air theatre, of an aviary and zoo, of steps to deals with one ugly iron wall and the residential quarters. In his reference to a synthetic system of inter-related Colleges (to deflect the danger of imagining all this to be a 'one-man show'), we now have an addition which he had not mentioned before – of Medicine, which does come as a surprise from Geddes. The mystery is cleared in a later letter from Montpellier in which he refers to the possibility of a Medical Village with his notes and work on the Tower, on Civilization courses, Regional Survey, Art and Environment. In this section of the correspondence, we note how Arthur is enjoying his work and its challenges and how he has blended in, in spite of the basic living standards and the dry, long hot months of Birbhum district! Moreover, we see echoes of his father's international examples being tried out in his teaching at Sriniketan with encouraging results as he uses Frank Mears' Palestine diagram of olive terraces drying up in his nature study class, which his boys, familiar with the drought problem, soon grasp. Arthur has given talks on Geddes' theory of the inter-related interests of Place, Work and Folk, which were received in a 'keen way' by his audience. Arthur is convinced that if Geddes drew his salary from lecturing at Shantiniketan rather than at Bombay, his ideas would be accepted and his experiments see fulfilment. One wishes it had happened!

We also confront conflicting forces in two figures whom Tagore (and Andrews, from his feeble support of them) respected and encouraged. There was the artist, Nanda Lal Bose, who was in charge of Visva-Bharati's

---

66 Boardman, 1944, p. 398.

Fine Arts College (Kala Bhavan) and the architect, to whom Geddes probably refers as the 'shocking Amateur Architect of Art School' and asks as to whether he is 'now retrained', after his '5 blots of wasteful architecture'. One wonders if this is a reference to Suren Kar, and, what were these '5 blots'? They could not be the Uttarayan complex as it was not completed when Geddes wrote this particular letter. Suren Kar, with Rathindranath, designed, built and extended, in a long period between 1921 and 1938, the five buildings of the Uttarayan complex that formed Rabindranath Tagore's residential quarters, as the poet moved restlessly from one building to the other. The delay in completing the construction shows the fickleness of the nature of funding pouring into Shantiniketan. Of Suren Kar, Dutta and Robinson say he was 'a painter on the staff with a talent for inexpensive and somewhat fanciful architecture; Kar designed most of the buildings in Shantiniketan, borrowing elements from Hindu temples, Mughal and Rajput palaces and from Java and Japan'.[67] The buildings are, as Geddes says, 'fanciful' in their eastern appeal, and the fact that Tagore had each one built when he felt dissatisfied with the one he was in, could be attributed to either their structure or to a poet's eternal restlessness!

Tagore and Geddes agreed on Branford's *Science and Sanctity* and its 'idealism and reconstructive vision and aim', which is evidenced in Tagore's request to Geddes to review it for the *Visva-Bharati Quarterly*, with which Geddes complies.[68] In his letter Andrews says how Tagore found his 'Report' (Indore) 'good', 'original' and 'refreshing'. He goes on to comment on Tagore's own translation of Visva-Bharati as University, which he feels, does not do ample justice to his ideal of a 'settlement' where people come to live a life and form 'a *kind of laboratory of great thinking – living out as far as they can what they are thinking*'. Perhaps at one time this was the 'university ideal itself'. Andrews is convinced 'that the "Ashram" of Ancient India is always in the Poet's mind' (17 January 1924). This brings to mind Israel Zangwill's description of Geddes' Outlook Tower: 'it was *a sociological laboratory*, it was *a meeting place* for all those *who had common interests in the community* or in the *intellectual life* …'[69] (italics my own).

---

[67] Dutta and Robinson, 1995, p. 330.

[68] See Patrick Geddes 'Education and Reconstruction: A Review', *Visva-Bharati Quarterly*, April 1924 (Bengali: Vaisakh, 1331).

[69] Preface, in Defries, 1927, p. 6.

Even after Geddes left India, his intellectual exchange with Tagore continued as Geddes settled down in the friendlier climate of Montpellier to develop the Scots College and his dream of an Indian College. In 1925 he requests Tagore to accept the position of President of the first 'International Congress on University Progress', which Tagore does, and Geddes asks him to address them and to be a delegate with Geddes in the 'World Conference in Education' to speak on their respective institutions. Both Congresses were to be held in Edinburgh in the last week of July. The intellectual comradeship in forging and framing new frontiers in higher education is thus sought and hopes are raised by Tagore's full acquiescence to Geddes' proposals. The possibility of interaction between kindred International Institutions (i.e., at Montpellier, Visva-Bharati and Jerusalem), is also broached in another request to Tagore to add his name to a joint message of goodwill in line with Tagore's own 'message of mutual tolerance' at Jerusalem University. The humanism that Tagore admired so much in Geddes, as he said in his foreword, is evident in these endeavours to bring about communal and racial harmony through educational institutions with universal programmes. Geddes also expands on the ideal environment of Montpellier for a student, promising an 'effective' and 'more meditative life', to build the body, mind and spirit and so parallels Tagore's idea of the Ashram.

Tagore's heart problem intervenes and Geddes has the 'Conference of University Progress' postponed till Tagore's next visit to Europe. This is just the beginning of thwarted hopes as successive invitations sent by Geddes to Tagore to come and give his 'benefaction' to the students at Montpellier cannot be honoured as plans and journeys are curtailed by the relapses in Tagore's illness.

Geddes remains an inspiration even in his absence as Andrews prepares to take his geography students to experience and survey the landscape and witness the effect of erosion 'during the rains in our laterite soil'. As Geddes sees the opening of his university building at Jerusalem, later in the same year, i.e., in 1925, Arthur's plan for the 'Tata Building' sees fruition in a construction that would certainly have had Geddes' approval in being on a prospect and 'wonderfully breezy and cool' to suit the burning days of long summers at Shantiniketan.

The same year Geddes writes to Tagore about the Industrial progress of Western civilization which has led to War and its aftermath,[70] in which the mechanistic, numerical (pecuniary) has been paramount, giving rise to a 'Utilitarian (pseudo)-philosophy, which has proved – in a very Geddesian term – 'futilitarian'. Now, for the first time, he mentions the need for a 'Synthetic Movement', from mechanistic ('analytical treatment of science') to 'harmonized sciences', as he explains – a 'higher science of life', in its 'application to education, industry and life'.[71] Geddes deplores the lack of synthesis in universities from medieval to modern Science Institutes. He also deplores the examination system prevailing at universities. In a previous letter to Arthur he had referred to them as 'cramshops'. Tagore shares the same irreverence for university examinations. As mentioned earlier, they were suspicious of university establishments and neither of them took university degrees.

Arthur continues the strong ties he had established with Tagore at Shantiniketan, whom he now addresses as 'Gurudev' in letters exchanged with the poet. He discusses the compilation of thirty of Tagore's songs (fifteen from 'The King of the Dark Chamber' and fifteen 'Spring Tunes'). Tagore's affection for Arthur and his reliance on his ability, judgement and integrity are evident in his *carte blanche* to him, 'Do whatever you like with my songs' and in his permission to write the accompaniments, 'I trust you, for you are modest' and in the confidence he has in him in that he will not

---

[70] Geddes and Tagore, as advocates of peace, were against war. When Geddes won the first prize for Cities Exhibition at Congress of Cities in Ghent in 1913, the second position went to an 'elaborate German exhibit. Given the rising tensions in 1913 between the two nations, this victory was hailed by some as a striking triumph for Britain. But Geddes was anxious to get beyond national rivalries...' His response was characteristic of the international responsible intellectual, reaching out beyond nationalistic boundaries, 'the present main struggle for existence is not that of fleets and armies, but between the Paleotechnic and Neotechnic order.' Marshall Stalley ed. with an Introduction, *Patrick Geddes: Spokesman for Man and the Environment: A Selection* (New Brunswick, New Jersey: Rutgers University Press, 1972) pp. 70, 71.
Tagore's strong views against the War and his deep sadness are evident in the many lectures and talks he gave in the West and the East.

[71] 'Geddes advocated such breadth of vision at a time when specialization was getting into its mechanical stride (soon to be supported by the requirements of two world wars) with the consequences of restriction of thought and action and environmental depredation with which we are now familiar. He saw educational and environmental problems with clarity where few others could see them, and this, combined with his untimely generalism (thoughtless of Geddes to be so hard to classify), may explain his relative neglect.' Macdonald, 1992, pp. 118-119. Tagore says 'The most important branch of secular knowledge is the science of life...' 'The Unity of Education' in Kabir, 1961, p. 236.

'smother' his 'tunes' with his own embellishments. Tagore promises not verse translations but prose translations in English for the songs, in these attempts of Arthur to bring the East to the West. The songs did not see the light of publication before Tagore's death, and his daughter has given me a compilation of fourteen of them instead of the thirty that Arthur writes about.

Geddes continues to plan and progress, setting forth the international attraction of Montpellier and still hoping that amidst its buildings and gardens, which he is sure Tagore will like, they will have 'that long-delayed talk'. No rancour here or the reservations expressed at the late arrival of the Plan in February 1923 to Mahalanobis! Geddes requests on behalf of all at Montpellier, that Tagore, as 'an admirable and spiritual musician, a true idealist' should write a song for 'expressing the movement of international sympathy' for them. Tagore would love to comply, but he jokes about the English Muse eluding him, which would have to be the language of such a song. A poem arrives in 1929 – the long-awaited 'benediction' for Geddes' Indian College, not for its foundation stone, as it comes the following year. It will be put on the Memorial stone as the building for the Indian College is nearly complete now and Tagore is still unable to come on account of his poor health.

Geddes tells Tagore how 'The Parrot's Training' has delighted people in France and asks for the illustration blocks for a French translation, which shows how this allegorical story of Tagore has, with Geddes' recommendation of it, struck international chords.

There are five Indian students at various stages of completing their theses at Montpellier, along with Arthur and another to join them from the Edinburgh Outlook Tower. In fact, Arthur writes to Rathindranath around this time about his thesis on Bengal's 'soil and civilization' which he would like to go over with Tagore and Rathindranath. Geddes asks Tagore to foster the international scope of the College by sending some of his students – or even one – hoping that the 'examples' such a student brings with him, 'of Surul and surrounding villages will awaken the greatest of Mediterranean Schools of Agriculture'. The topic of Arthur's research reinforces his links with Bengal. In all these letters to Tagore, there is a case made for Montpellier as the ideal place for a student to come to, rather than face the shock of an Oxford, a Cambridge... for 'here are definite beginnings of interest to you – and even with bearings of Shantiniketan and its planning....'[72] Tagore asks for the costs an Indian student will have to bear, towards which Geddes hopes to raise funds. He will seek such students to 'give an international atmosphere' to the place and asks if Arthur can write a detailed description of Montpellier for the *Modern Review*. So we see the international communication finding fresh expression and the promise of a scope for future expanding exchanges. It is at this time that Geddes speaks about working towards a League of Academic Nations to which he has been a great contributor in assisting in the planning of three international institutions at Jerusalem, Shantiniketan and Montpellier. Here, what he has achieved is to promote 'science in definite co-operation with "humanities" and socialized applications – from city to village renewal... from horticulture to agriculture to... afforestation...' There are letters and telegrams (I do not include the latter) written/sent by Tagore, Geddes, Arthur, Rathindranath, Elmhirst and even J.C. Bose (whose letter to Geddes of 17th November 1926 is not included in this collection, but it is pertinent to note that he does say that Tagore is probably in Germany when he writes, probably following up an enquiry of Geddes'). This volley of letters is cut short by Tagore's illness and return to Shantiniketan, to be picked up again in the same crescendo of rising hopes of Tagore's visit to Montpellier in 1928 when Tagore comes to deliver the Hibbert Lectures at Oxford.[73] The hopes are dashed when he falls ill and has to return to India.

Geddes' letter to Tagore of 1927 shows the undaunted fortitude of the education theorist. He sends his famous sketch of the three doves, symbolizing 'Sympathy, Synergy' (a quality Geddes himself possesses to the utter amazement of his associates who could not keep up with this chain reaction of self-generating energy), and 'Synthesis' – standing for 'Heart, Hand and Head' – the 'Good, Beautiful and True', to establish a 'Studia Synthesis' interacting and in harmony with 'Agenda Synergica'. Geddes was then seventy-three and still a creative visionary! He has a whole new agenda

---

[72] In 'A Poet's School' Tagore says of Shantiniketan, 'We have only made a beginning. We have given the children an opportunity to find their freedom in nature by being able to love it.' Kabir, 1961, p. 296.

[73] The Hibbert Lectures were published as 'The Religion of Man' by Allen and Unwin and dedicated to Dorothy Elmhirst. Also in Sisir Kumar Das, *The English Writings of Rabindranath Tagore: A Miscellany* (New Delhi: Rabindra-Bhavana, Sahitya Akaedmy, 1996) Vol Three, pp. 83-189.

for the better organisation of universities, encompassing disciplines,[74] nomenclature and library systems. He reiterates his life-long ideas of seeing science established in close association with man's occupations, having 'orderly studies' in institutions with 'small beginnings but large principles',[75] existing not in 'academic groupings' but activating 'substantial unity and harmony', a 'Vita Sympathetica' sending an 'impulse of cooperative activities... extending from individual friendships and social harmonies, and to racial sympathies'.[76] Such was the vision both Tagore and Geddes shared, succeeding in small beginnings, working towards that League of Academic Nations (United Academic Nations?) with their message of universal peace symbolized in Geddes' three doves and Tagore's Shantiniketan – the abode of peace.

In 1929, Geddes again writes to Tagore, anticipating his visit to Montpellier next year, on Tagore's trip to Europe to deliver the once postponed Hibbert Lectures. He has reread 'Creative Unity' of Tagore's with fresh and renewed appreciation. This essay ('The Religion of the Forest') discusses the message of the forest and the ideal of the *tapovana* which Tagore revived at Shantiniketan. He is still sure that the right way to forge understanding, is for Tagore to send a student to Montpellier, thus 'bringing together the East and West'.[77] He gives the example of German scholar Dr. Stressman, who, having studied in Geneva with its French culture, could appreciate it and not hate it, contrary to the general attitude

---

[74] He had conceived of this years earlier from 1887, when he organized and held the famous Summer Meetings at Edinburgh. 'The motto of [these] ... Meetings was Vivendo Discimus – By Living We Learn – and therefore, reasoned P.G., what better way is there of learning something new than by taking part in actual life as people live it? Secondly, he held before both teachers and students one goal: to reunite the separate studies of art, of literature, and of science into a related cultural whole which should serve as an example to the universities still mainly engaged in breaking knowledge up into particles unconnected with each other or with life.' Introduction, Lewis Mumford in Boardman, 1944, p. 157.

[75] See the footnote 68 regarding Tagore's own description of his efforts in founding a school at Shantiniketan. Geddes' ideal matches the ancient Indian ideal adopted at Shantiniketan of plain living and high thinking, which, as we know, is both Ruskinian and Gandhian and in alignment with the basic principles of the Enlightenment.

[76] Tagore too was an optimist. He says, '...it is being proved that the positive force which works at the basis of natural selection is the power of sympathy, the power to combine. In the nineteenth century, the message of political economy was unrestrained competition; in the twentieth, it is beginning to change into co-operation.' 'The Centre of Indian Culture' in Kabir, 1961, p.218.

[77] Tagore nurtured the same belief. He has said, 'I refuse to think that the twin spirits of East and West, the Mary and the Martha, can never meet to make perfect the realization of truth. And in spite of our material poverty and the antagonism of time I wait patiently for this meeting.' 'A Poet's School' in Kabir, 1961, p. 295.

of 'Prussians'. He again reiterates the benevolent efficacy of a living and biologic science, rather than a 'mechanistic, pecuniary' one, which Tagore will witness at Montpellier, 'you see your example of Surul is having its effect beyond its immediate range'.[78] This is the international cooperation that Tagore and Geddes effected and wished to have continue in their absence. Tagore believed that villages could only prosper and thrive through co-operative ventures which he effectively put into practise on his father's estate at Shelidah and again through Sriniketan, in the surrounding villages.[79] Both Tagore and Geddes were against 'Militant' science, which Tagore considered a misdirected application of science for material exploitation, which inevitably leads to aggrandisement and war.[80]

---

[78] For Geddes 'Education is not merely by and for the sake of thought; it is in a still higher degree by and for the sake of action... For it is only by thinking things out as one lives them, and by living things out as one thinks them, that a man or society can really be said to think or even live at all". Thus, whether in botany or in literature, the student was urged to get beyond the destructive analysis of flowers or verse and achieve some measure of constructive synthesis... artistic study of the human figure was related to anthropology and history, study of landscapes to geology, the study of society to language and literature ... In short, the scientist worked for the artist, the artist for the scientist, and the man of letters for both. 'In a word, we learn by living!' Boardman, 1944, p. 159.

And Tagore notes that '...our life, our thought and our language are not harmonized. Because of this fundamental disunity, we cannot stand on our feet, cannot get what we want, cannot succeed in our efforts'. 'The Vicissitudes of Education', p. 48. Elsewhere he says, 'For true education is to realize at every step how our training and knowledge have an organic connection with our surroundings'. 'The Centre of Indian Culture', p. 203. 'I tried to create an atmosphere in my school – this was the main task. In educational institutions our faculties have to be nourished in order to give our mind its freedom, to make our imagination fit for the world which belongs to art, and to stir our sympathy for human surroundings. This last is even more important than learning the geography of foreign lands.' 'A Poet's School' in Kabir, 1961, p. 300.

Elsewhere he says, 'Cities have their functions of maintaining wealth and knowledge in concentrated forms of opulence, but this... should not be for their own sake; they should be centres of irrigation; they should gather in order to distribute... Such a relationship of mutual benefit between the city and the village can remain strong only so long as the spirit of cooperation and self-sacrifice is a living ideal in society... (destroying the dichotomy of 'exploiter and victim')... We have started... with our Visva-Bharati, work of village re-construction, the mission of which is to retard the process of race suicide... 'City and Village' in Kabir, 1961, p. 226.

[79] See Tagore's essays, 'City and Village' and 'Society and State', Kabir, 1961, pp. 302-322, pp. 49-66.

[80] In his deep conviction that War could not achieve an ideal world, Geddes said in a letter to his son Alasdair in early August, 1914, 'The war is not a crusade of new ideals but a Gadarene rout of dying ideas and ideals, the legions of Devils of the past entering into the people and driving them to ruin... Here are the mechanical and the romantic ideas of the paleotects, the jingoism of the imperialists and their bureaucracies, the protests of the Socialists, the great doings of the financiers and the anarchic discontent they especially create.' Boardman, 1978, p. 249. [continued on next page]

We see Geddes denouncing the 'Militant pseudo civilization of the Industrial Age' and advocating the move towards 'Life-teaching',[81] which would, through rural regenerative action ensure 'some further harmony of East and West.' This humanistic approach of a scientist is explained by Geddes in his description of Boshi Sen's science as 'vitalized, moralized, socialized, and even religionized'.[82]

The letterhead around this time, shows Tagore as President and Dr. J.C. Bose as Vice President of the Indian College. References show that there were other letters which have been lost. With two succeeding letters, Geddes sends Tagore some of his papers, on 'Wealth versus Thought', 'Current Progress... and the Plague of the Pre-War Mind', on 'Pro-Synthesis', on the 'mechanical' to the 'vital' and on 'Social Transition', which all show how this fountain of ideas continues to overflow in one developing, active chain of sincere conviction, which he shares with Tagore. This is evidence of the fact that he knows that he is understood by an Indian (apart from the other Indian, Dr. J.C. Bose). The link is clinched and carved in stone as it were, as Geddes' Edinburgh architect, without his influence, has carved the Ashoka pillar at the corner of the Tower of the Indian College, to record a meeting of East and West in an Indian College in a European country, showing that two minds had indeed 'met'.

Tagore has evidently sought Geddes' advice and Geddes urges him to write of his Shantiniketan school and of Visva-Bharati to spread his 'impulse to education over the wide world' and to keep a documentary evidence of his 'initiative' for his successors to continue developing.

'He denounced the war-like, jingoistic spirit that pervaded Britain towards the end of the nineteenth century, and tried to show how the technical advances of the industrial revolution should be used for home peace, not armed forces and war.' Kitchen, 1975, p. 22. In 1917, Geddes was to lose this much loved and valued son, in the War.

And Tagore has said, '... it is all too obvious that nations are coming together without uniting – and the agony of it afflicts the world today... Nations have grown by the power of truth, but not nationalism. ... It is a national folly, this deadly passion for self-aggrandizement that makes people averse to international unity. 'The Unity of Education' in Kabir, 1961, p. 248.

[81] P. Kitchen said that it is unfortunate that the most positive term coined by Geddes, ['world-mending'] 'geotechnics' should not have been accepted by the English language. Another word which could well have been picked up by the world, is biotechnics, which explains Geddes' [and Tagore's...] idea of Life-teaching. Kitchen, 1975, p. 24.

[82] Tagore shares similar ideas of the inspired teacher: 'even in our attempts to found national universities we begin from the wrong end. The students come first, and then we cast about for the teachers.' 'The Centre for Indian Culture', in Kabir, 1961, p. 213. For similar thoughts, see Tagore's 'The Religion of the Forest' in Das, 1996, Vol. Two, pp. 511-19.

One interesting coincidence emerges. The Indian College is the gift of 'Sir Ratan Tata Trustees'. Some years ago, Andrews has referred to the great success of the 'Tata Building', which was a fruit of Arthur's plan, at Shantiniketan. Both friends have found the same patron for educational ventures.

Geddes' friend, Thomas Barclay, in arranging a lunch for Tagore at the Institute of 'Cooperation Intellectual' states that 'The nationalist-reactionaries would no doubt like to enlist him as an enemy of England, but I am sure there is no more earnest votary for peace than a man who is one of the glories of British civilization... he represents not one country but civilization common to all cultures' – vouching for the universal man in Tagore – and the second section (from 'but...') could well apply to Geddes.

Geddes' wish for Tagore to lecture in Edinburgh on 'What's wrong with Scotland', shows the absence of sectarian politics in a man who could look objectively at his own country which he loved, as his work in slum regeneration at Edinburgh, his gardens at University College in Dundee and his meticulously prepared Report for Dunfermline, illustrate.

The last recorded letter from Geddes to Tagore in April 1930 in this volume, shows how 'sorely grieved' he is – not at Tagore's failure to come to Montpellier as the President – but for the 'interruption [owing to the relapse of Tagore's heart problem] of your splendid progress through the world, which despite all its drawbacks, [is] ever widening, quickening, awakening to your message'. And Geddes' last message is that Neotechnic/Modern man,[83] striving for 'vital' science for 'social use and service', would ensure the reappearance of 'little bits of Cosmos' in the small beginnings of Shantiniketan, Visva-Bharati, the Outlook Tower in Edinburgh and the Scots College with its Indian College at Montpellier, which could become a regenerative force for the world and in its cooperative future, Indian. There is a note by Geddes at the top right-hand corner of the letter, saying 'not yet sent'. We hope it was sent to a sad and ailing Tagore, from a much valued friend.

---

[83] Geddes' 'distinction between the first, crude phase of the Industrial Age – 'the Paleotechnic' and the more efficient, cleaner, less life-destroying 'Neotechnic' phase, has been justified by its advances for a century past. And surely a growing care for life is justifying his prevision of a Biotechnic leading to a Eutechnic phase.' (Introduction, Arthur Geddes, Mairet, 1957), p.xix.

After an understandable silence, following Geddes' death, Arthur re-establishes the link with Tagore, asking Tagore, if he will give his name to an accompanying letter to the Principal as his consent to a wish to let Arthur continue the work his father was doing, of which Tagore 'heartily approves'. Arthur adds that he has written, apart from his geographical books (including the one on Bengal), another work, 'Spirit of the Tartan', which he says, would not have been possible if he had not heard and seen Tagore's dramas, *Sacrifice*, the *Dark Chamber* and the *Spring Tune* – just as, years before, Tagore's adaptation of Burns' songs in Bengali would not have found a fresh impetus if Tagore had not, perhaps, heard Arthur playing and singing his Scottish airs.

The last word, in this collection, is (and rightly so), Arthur's, talking about developing a scheme of 'travelling geographers' as Tagore had envisaged, after the first step of 'mix[ing] minds' as he has done at Shantiniketan and Geddes did in his Summer Meetings at Edinburgh and tried to initiate at Montpellier and at Jerusalem, and then to send 'an embassy of learners' out. This letter shows that Tagore's influence on Geddes' son was profound. In the same vein, Geddes' influence on the next generation across the world was no less potent, as Tagore's son, Rathindranath, had said earlier, 'let us not do anything without a plan!' inspired as he had been by Geddes' method of forging development with visionary plans.

Whether the two men met as frequently as they wanted to, or whether the much desired 'business' talk ever took place or not, are questions not worth considering now. The letters are important today in this very divided world because of the ideas they express and the philosophy behind the educational institutions that Tagore and Geddes did so much to conceive and build up – all of which comes across so expressively in this correspondence.

Bashabi Fraser
Centre for South Asian Studies
Edinburgh University

Above   Patrick Geddes with members of his class, c. 1919
Below   Patrick Geddes and his planning assistant, Indore, India, c. 1919

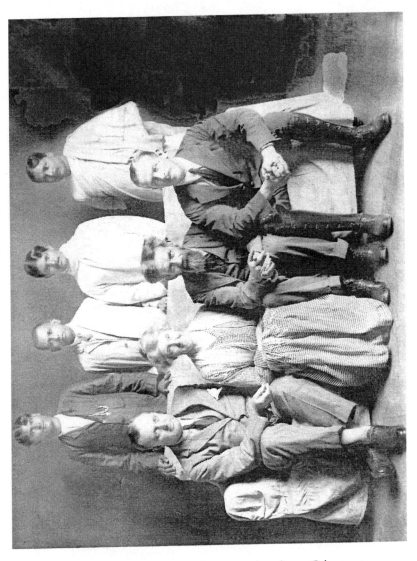

Patrick Geddes, his wife, Anna, colleagues and students, Calcutta, 1915

Above	Tagore in Karachi, 1923
Opposite, above	Tagore in Japan, 1916
	probably with Pearson and C.F. Andrews
Opposite, below	Tagore with Gandhiji

Tagore as Balmiki in his dance drama *Balmiki Pratibha*

Rathindranath Tagore, the poet's son

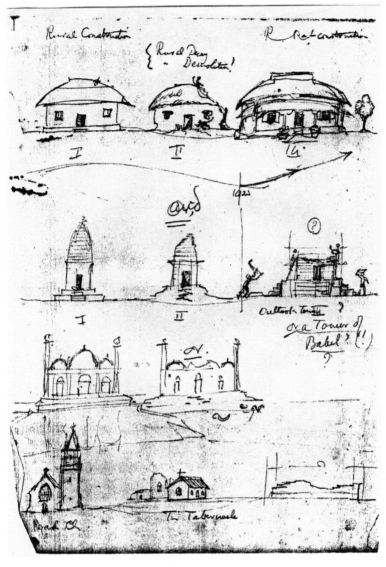

Above   Arthur's sketch page

Opposite, above Arthur Geddes as 'Gurudev' knew him, 1922
Opposite, below Arthur Geddes in India, 1956

Above   Signed photograph of Rev. C.F. Andrews

Opposite, above The old library at Shantiniketan
Opposite, below Surul Kuthi (Kuthi means 'building' in Bengali)

Above Rural Reconstruction Office
Below Udayan, Tagore's residence at Shantiniketan. There are five
distinctive buildings in the complex, and the poet moved from one to the
other according to the time of year and his prevailing mood. Gandhi's
favourite was the mud hut called 'Shyamali'.

Above The Scots College founded by Patrick Geddes at Montpellier
Below The Indian College founded by Patrick Geddes at Montpellier of
which Rabindranath Tagore was the President and Sir Jagadish Chandra
Bose was Vice President.

Shelida *(sic)*, Nadia
16 February 1914

Dear Mr. Young,

I am glad that you enjoyed your visit to our Ashram. My only regret is that some of us were absent and the school was not in full swing – but you have met Kalimohan, and through him known what ideas our Asram represents. However, I hope you will have occasions to come to us often when Willie settles down to this place, and give us opportunity to know you all as our friends. Do not imagine me among the quivering shadows of our sal trees busy shedding old leaves and putting on new ones. I am floating down the Ganges in a boat while the post office is waving its letter bags in vain from the banks.

Yours sincerely
Rabindranath Tagore

The Manor House
Britford
NR. Salisbury

14 December 1914

Dear Mrs. Geddes,

I should have written before, but had to remain a few days in London and during the weekend we had a visitor. Now I thank you very sincerely for your kind hospitality, which added greatly to the pleasure of my stay in Edinburgh. Please tell Mrs. Padmore that I did not fail to call on the Basus. I am at last returning the Helundis *(sic)* book: and as you suggest I send a copy of your book to Mrs. Kennedy Fraser, which you perhaps will not mind forwarding? With very kind regards

Yours sincerely,
Ananda Coomaraswamy.

To Anna Geddes

Charles Freer Andrews
Writer on India

27, Fitzroy Square, W
16 December 1914

The Rev. C.F. Andrews
Delhi

Dear Mr. Andrews,

Though I had only the pleasure of meeting you for few minutes (when you were good enough to call on me at Mr. Haley's camp) I hope you may remember me, and that you will allow me to introduce you to my old friend Professor Patrick Geddes, whose work as a biologist and sociologist is no doubt familiar to you. I am sure that no one can help Professor Geddes better than you can to see the right things and people in India and to see them in the right way.

Yours very truly
William Archer

27, Fitzroy Square, W.
16 December 1914

Dear Mrs. Naidu,

This is to introduce you – if you do not know him already – Professor Patrick Geddes, a very eminent sociologist and one of my oldest friends. It would be a misfortune to both of you if he were to leave India without making your acquaintance.

We talk of you often and wonder how you are and where and how Mr. Naidu is. If he has actually come to Europe, I hope very much that we may see him before he returns.

Yours very sincerely
William Archer

Dear Mr. Young,

You may thank your lucky stars that your book is safe. Contrary to his custom Andrews not only lent it to me but also gave me instruction to send it back to its rightful owner – which I hasten to carry out with thanks to you. I have read this book with very great pleasure as I am in perfect agreement with most of the ideas contained in it. Some of my American lectures have their full support in this book in a remarkable measure.

I haven't received a line from Pearson since my return to India. He has deliberately taken a plunge into obscurity, which post office cannot fathom. But I have his assurance that he would be back about the middle of June.

I suppose you know that Andrews is about to start for Fiji. I wish it were possible for him to take rest which he needs more than anything else.

With best regards

Very sincerely

Yours
Rabindranath Tagore

Bettia
Champaran
5 *(sic)* May 1917[84]

Dear Mr. Young,

I thank you for your letter. No apology was needed for it. I don't think the commissioner was much to blame, if at all. He could do no otherwise than act upon the reports of his friends. The planters' influence is tremendous *(sic)* here. And he took their word that my object was agitation *(sic)*.

I know the factory evil throughout India. But I have not been able to study it. There is moreover a world of difference between what happens here and in the ordinary factories. The latter only control their labourers who are wretchedly kept in houses, the former demands and receives the service and money of their so-called tenants.

Yours sincerely,
M K Gandhi

---

[84] Gandhi was in Champaran in 1917, accompanying the peasant sharecropper Rajkumar Shukla, to investigate Shukla's complaint about the landlord system in Bihar. He arrived in April 1917 at Tagore's school at Shantiniketan, where he stayed two days, from where he proceeded to Champaran. One can assume that this letter was probably written that year. He stayed for seven months at Champaran and paid several shorter visits later. See Louis Fischer, *The Life of Mahatma Gandhi* (London: Granada, 1982).

Ahmedabad

30 June 1917[85]

Dear Mr. Young,

I value your letter. I know that we cannot entirely get rid of *(sic)* machinery. But different results flow from two different positions – one that welcomes machines as a blessing and the other which recognising it as an evil tolerates it when it must. We would agree to *(sic)* principles if you accept the proposition that a state in which machinery is least used is the happier for it.

The question of [illegible] we shall discuss when we meet some day. I hope to see you one of these days passing a vacation in a part of it according as it suits you.

Yours sincerely,

M K Gandhi

---

[85] Again, following Gandhi's biographical details, this was probably written in 1917. Fisher writes, 'Gandhi would have remained to assist the sharecroppers of Champaran (further)… but unrest among textile workers brought him back to Ahmedabad.' (Fischer, 1951), p. 197. Moreover, Tagore's letter to Mr. Young of 26 April 1917 refers to Andrews' forthcoming trip for Fiji which tallies with Fischer's reference to Gandhi's meeting with Andrews at Champaran, prior to his departure for Fiji. Ibid., p. 196.

Dear Sir Rabindranath,

Admirable! The parrot is being avenged! – and what is yet better, future parrots will be protected! rescued, [illegible][86] It would have pleased you – the delight with which my friend C.E. Dobson here, Rector of the big High School (1500 boys – far too many) carried off this and gloated over it; & showed it to the very people it is meant to kill! – (or cure?)

I am sure it will help the cause everywhere.

Even the weakness of our hesitating yet would-be friends is due to the feeling that Indians want the poorest treatment, because people like Sadhu do. A converse opinion has now to be stirred to expression. So pray continue to fight – now – before the Commission furnishes its report this month at Darjeeling, & then takes it to Simla (to be watered down by reactionaries, I fear, there!)

Yours always cordially

P Geddes

With such caricaturists to help you there is a great field of action – Go on! There is a time for War; and this is it! I am writing to Thacker to ask him terms for 250 – 500 copies to send through Universities and Colleges etc through Europe and USA!

I have only delayed replying promptly, to send you extract reprint of my report here on "proposed University". I have got 500 copies, and shall send to any you suggest. Pray do let you see send me a list. *(sic)* My feeling and hope are that these simultaneous appearances, yet totally different and independent attacks may help each other in various minds.

---

[86] There are two words that are not legible.

Thus Dr. Sadhu etc. of University Committee for CU are far more with us than you perhaps realise. Do send them copies! (Address c/o Govt. House Darjeeling) I am of course sending him all I write, and he was delighted with my Evidence of which I read you part at Bolpur – So all this will give them more courage.

Santiniketan
15 June 1918

Dear Professor,

I have sent a copy of 'Parrot's Training' to Dr. Sadhu. He had already read it when it appeared in the Modern Review and expressed his enthusiastic appreciation of it in a letter to the Editor. Sometime ago he spent a night here in our school when I had an opportunity of long conversations with him. I was delighted to find that in all vital things about education we agreed. But I am afraid the commission is composed of members most of whom differ in their views from Dr. Sadhu – and the people are already explaining their doubt about the result. What we need now is an ideal university in some of our Native States. A few months ago I received a letter from the Nizam State asking my opinion about the advisability of introducing Urdu to be the medium of instruction in a new university they intend to start. Do you know anything about it? I do hope you will be able to purchase some of our ruling chiefs to give Education a freer scope.

Please send me twenty copies of your Report which I will distribute among men who are interested.

Yours very sincerely

Rabindranath Tagore

Town Planning Office
Chiman Bagh Indore
26 June 1918

Dear Sir Rabindranath,

Herewith at last I send you my contribution to the Parrot's Freedom, which I hope you'll give me your criticism of some time at leisure.

Also the 20 copies for your friends. I have sent to Dr. Sadhu and his colleagues. And I suppose you'll give one of these to the Editor of the Modern Review. If you wish any more let me know, and send me addresses.

As to Hyderabad University it is beginning badly. At Lucknow I made the acquaintance of one of the (too few) Moslem intellectuals, Abdul Majid, a writer on psychology. He was opposite Professor at Hyderabad and thought he had at last got the chance of his life – Urdu & all : but alas. the "Director of Education" put him and his colleagues into a "Translation Bureau" – to turn into Urdu the bad textbooks of his own youth – exactly the scribe of your brother's picture (– opposite which I have put in his letter!) In addition to this, the Holy Moslem Inquisition looks after them all with peculiar rigour! Is it not pitiable!

It might help the University here if you can send a letter which the Maharajas and Ministers might read to any one here. I have made some impression here & there – though not, I fear, much.

Do you know the Chief of Udaipur? (I am going there for a holiday I think next week.) My point in the paper is that it is not by founding colleges which are at present doomed to pre-Germanic forms, and will need [illegible] at best only get from Commission a little sub-Germanic freedom – but by founding free Institutes and Libraries and Outlooks of Initiation too – that the beginnings of the Free and Reconstructive University Militant can be made most readily and without the huge expense and loss and disappointment of the present method.

Yours cordially
P Geddes.

GEDDES AND COLLEAGUES
Town Planners, Park and Garden
Designers, Museum Planners, etc.

OUTLOOK TOWER, EDINBURGH.
MORE'S GARDEN, CHELSEA. S.W.
TOWN PLANNING OFFICE, CALCUTTA

_____

CITY SURVEYS AND REPORTS
CITY PLANS AND IMPROVEMENTS

GARDEN SUBURBS AND VILLAGES
PARKS AND GARDENS

UNIVERSITY AND COLLEGE BUILDINGS, HOSTELS, etc.
TYPE MUSEUMS

EXHIBITIONS:–
    THE CIVIC EXHIBITION
    of Cities and Town Planning
    DIRECTOR :– PROF. GEDDES

TOWN PLANNING OFFICE[87]

Calcutta,

1 April 1919

Dear Sir Rabindranath,

Congratulations on your lectures on "Education", & on "<u>Forest</u>" here, each so fine in its way. I hope you'll <u>erupt</u> again over the Calcutta University Commission question and other things. (Don't you even sing better after a hard battle, like the warrior of old?) (And pray make your publisher send a good packet of Parrot's Training to England, where as needed).

I have been writing a "Life of Bose", in which his service and some of his battles too are set forth. He will send it you when published (I trust with Autumn season by Longmans).

_____

[87] This is the letterhead.

60

Young B. Ganguly has made me a good sketch of Bose for a frontispiece, – better than any photo, of course. He would like to sketch you too some day – will you allow him? – I give him this to send on to you, as I shall be gone – till autumn at least – sailing on Tuesday.

Always very cordially – and appreciatively –

Yours

P Geddes.

4 August 1920

PS I have just written this about Dr. Patrick Geddes

What so strongly attracted me in Dr. Patrick Geddes when I came to know him in India was not his scientific achievements, but, on the contrary, the rare fact of the fulness of his personality rising far above his science. Whatever he has studied and mastered has become vitally one with his humanity. He has the precision of the scientist and the vision of the prophet, at the same time, the power of an artist to make his ideas visible through the language of symbols. His love of Man has given him the insight to see the truth of Man, and his imagination to realise in the world the infinite mystery of life and not merely its mechanical aspect.

Rabindranath Tagore

August. 4. 1920

Geneva
5 May 1921

Dear Geddes,

I am sorry for your not being able to come and for the cause of it. I hope that your friend is out of danger and your mind is at peace.[88]

I send you herewith a draft copy of an invitation letter from which you will know that I am arranging a conference of some representative men of the West and of Japan and China if possible. I wish to have your advice both with regards to names as well as the details of the programme. I need not say that it would help me greatly if you could personally take part in organising it. My scheme of the University has been well received in this country and I feel certain that I shall have volunteers who will join me from all parts of Europe. I have already received some very valuable offers of service. However, tell me how I am to proceed about this conference. Incidentally let me mention that I am willing to bear the travelling expenses of those for whom it is likely to be a burden. If you suggest any alterations in the wordings of the invitation letter I shall gratefully accept them. My intention is to hold in connection with the conference an exhibition representing different aspects of Indian life and culture.

Yours (illegible)

Rabindranath Tagore
c/o Dr. Hans Bodmer
Lesezirkel, Höttinggen, Zurich

---

[88] A reference to Victor Branford's illness.

The copy of the invitation letter[89]

You will know from the accompanying leaflet about the scheme of an International University in India with the object of paving the path to a future when both the East and West will work together for the general cause of human welfare. It has been decided formally to open this institution on the 15th of January, 1922, and to invite for the occasion a meeting of representative men and women of culture from the different countries of the West and from those in Asia which are likely to respond. Such a meeting of the best thinkers and workers who are interested in bringing about international good feelings and fellowship is sure to facilitate the communication of sympathy between these Continents which for various causes remain mutually alienated. It will give the most welcome assurance to the Eastern people that the best intellectual minds of the world recognise the claims of a common human birthright overcoming the barriers of geography and race. Earnestly hoping to count upon your sympathy for this movement I assure you that it will give me pleasure and strengthen the cause if you accept my invitation to take part in the conference affording the opportunity to some of our best men of distinction in India for meeting you.

---

[89] This letter is the 'draft copy of the invitation letter' referred to by Tagore in his letter of 5 May 1921 to Geddes.

Dear Tagore,

It was a pleasure to meet at Paris last summer, and a great regret that my engagements with my two home collaborators (Branford also being seriously ill, & Arthur Thomson not too well) prevented me from accepting your call to Geneva, which I would otherwise be delighted to do. But I have been getting on with my University planning, for Jerusalem etc.; first helped by stimulating contact with Paul Otlet etc. at the University International at Brussels, then with kindred beginnings at London and at my Outlook Tower at Edinburgh, but also especially last winter at Bombay. For there I have been fortunate in getting long galleries in the Institute of Science, and have thus not only installed my growing Library and <u>Dept of Sociology & Civics</u>, but my <u>Cities and Town Planning Exhibition</u> – a long picture book of cities (and their regions too in small measure) covering 1/4 mile and more of screens, crowded as close and high as may be, and outlining their past and present, and sometimes, their possible improvement too, as from Edinburgh to Jerusalem, and with something of Indian Cities also. (In fact very much of what I proposed to Mr. Tata 20 years ago when he was planning his big benefaction, and though then Sir William Ramsay managed to turn it all towards Chemistry and Physical Science, and at Bangalore, it is something to be able to express in Bombay, as <u>Gate to the West for India, and of India to the West</u>, how their respective cities may be studied and better understood in their qualities and defects, and with development of the one and domination of the other.)

But while I should like to show you this "picture-book", I think you would be more interested in the scheme of the associated Department, since not simply for its special theories and technical applications, but as also presenting in miniature, the mobilisation of the resources of the University. For what are all our arts and sciences, and how have they arisen, how too in progress? As drops of honey (sometimes tainted, alas with poison) from certain of the social lives of past and present. And how can we apply them better than towards mending the old lives, or starting the new as you are specially doing?

Consider the plan of this Department as miniature outline of the University's resources, applied towards clearer social thought, and better civic practice. For social science needs all that the preliminary sciences can teach it, and civics needs all the corresponding and independent arts. We need to be logical in our reasoning, and mathematical in our statistics and graphics, physical in our construction, biological in our agriculture, horticulture and hygiene, economic in our general undertakings: yet of all these sciences and arts, as you peculiarly and clearly see, (just as Ruskin saw before us or younger leaders now) are ineffective, when not <u>calamitous</u>, while expressing only the <u>sciences and arts of the material and mechanical order</u>, still so predominant, and so characteristic of the West. Poet and Artist, psychologist and educationist, moralist and mystic (and indeed even the traditionally religious) all necessarily see the crudeness, weakness and failure of such "science" and such "progress" – *(sic)* Yet they hardly do justice to the finer science, the truer progress for which some of us – Bose, Otlet, Paul Desjardins, and other mutual friends for example – are working. Consider then this diagram-plan of my department, with the various academic specialisms arranged, but now with <u>the subjective arts and sciences co-ordinated with these, and dominant accordingly</u>. Beginning first in the conventional academic way, which University men are ready for accordingly, (we shall come to your way, or at least nearer it, presently) – we have the essentials of

Logic   (as Science)
   "   (" Art)   evolving together as "thematic metrics"

Mathematics as Science
   "   (" Art, metrics, graphics, etc.)

Physics (energics)
Technics

Esthetics   "   "   "   Eutechnics
Fine Arts

Biology
Biotechnics (Agriculture Horticulture Medicine and Hygiene etc.)

| Psychology | " " " Psychorganics |
| Education | |

Economics	
Politics	
_____	" " " Etho-polity/ics
Ethics as Science	
" in practice (with Religions)	

But while the traditional University began with logic, (and thus too often stuck there, or now at various stages on the way Mathematical, Physical, etc) we now have to read upwards: – and in truer order, right hand first:- for the preceding technical terms but disguise for the moment, in our academic jargon, the world-old simplicity, since, unity of Life.

Life as "Conduct" ("Dharma" (Social) = Etho-polity, *i.e.*
Righteousness economics now at one, "duty" and
"Duty" etc) "efficiency" together the concave-
 convex of the same curve and thus
 inseparable.

Life as "Behaviour" (Individual) = Psychorganics; *i.e.* with
 psychology and biology – mind
 and body "sanity" and "health"
 together.

Life as "Activity" (Practical & applied = Eutechnics :
 in social service) *i.e.* with esthetics and physics,
 art and industries at one,
 "gesture" and "grasp" together.

If the preceding be clear, (uncongenial though may be the diagrammatic method and presentment, since this suspends any attempt at literary expression, – as mere foundation-plans lack architecture, yet I trust prepare for it) you will, I hope, agree that this is not the conventional and "hard shell" presentment of science, but at least contains a germ of the life we are all seeking, in however different ways.

66

(In my actual Department, the tables laid out all for the outlines of the arts face towards the City (in Exhibition), and those with outlines of the sciences face towards the library; yet on the opposite wall are brought together, and into the right order as above; *i.e.* from the "spiritual" to "temporal", from "transcendental" to "material and mechanical", or whatever other terms are preferred).

So far then the present attempt towards a step in University planning, which I am putting to Otlet, to Branford, and to my friends of the Jerusalem University. I should indeed be grateful if it turns out to be in harmony with your own vision; and so far as it falls short of this, I hope you will tell me.

Let me hear from you then, at leisure. I am here for another month or so, planning such improvements as may be for this old city, and for its College also, as also for one or two other towns of the state. After that my plans are uncertain. – I am tempted to return to Darjeeling, and sit down quietly to some writing there, (and learning too what I can from the unending wizardry of our friend Bose!) But I do not return to Bombay till the end of October.

Pardon this long letter (which has grown as I wrote!); and believe me, with all good wishes for your educational as well as other creative work, always very cordially yours, (and gratefully also,)

Pat. Geddes[90]

---

[90] There is a slight differences in this letter to the version at the National Library of Scotland, which ends with the paragraph 'So far then…University planning'.

Dear Geddes,

You ask me for my opinion about the scheme of your Department. I find it rather difficult to answer your question because my own work in Santiniketan has been from first to last a growth, which has had to meet all the obstacles and obstructions due to shortage of funds, paucity of workers, obtuseness in those who were called upon to carry out my ideal. But just because it was *a* living growth it has surmounted these difficulties and taken its own shape. In writing my stories, I hardly ever have a distinct plot in my mind. I start with some general emotional motive which goes on creating its story form, very often forgetting in the process its own original boundaries. If I had, in the commencement, a definite outline which I was merely to fill in, it would certainly bore me, – for I need the consistent stimulation of surprises, which comes only to a semi-passive medium through some living truth's gradual self-unfoldment.

The same thing happened with my Santiniketan Institution. I merely started with this one simple idea, that education should never be dissociated from life. I had no experience of teaching, no special gift for organisation; and therefore I had no plan which I could put before the public in order to win their confidence. I had not their power to anticipate what line my work was going to take. I began anyhow. All that I could do was to offer to the five little boys who were my first students my company. I talked and sang to them, played with them, recited to them our epics, improvised stories specially given to them by evening, took them on excursions into neighbouring villages.

It was an incessant lesson to me, and the institution grew with the growth of my own mind and life. With the increase of its population and the widening of its range, elements have constantly been intruding which go against its spirit of freedom and spontaneity. The consequent struggle has been helpful in strengthening and making us realise the fundamental truth which is in the heart of our ashram.

But that which keeps up my enthusiasm is the fact, that we have not yet come to a conclusion. And therefore our task is not a perpetual repetition of a plan perfected once for all.

My first idea was to emancipate children's minds from the dead grip of a mechanical method and a narrow purpose. This idea has gone on developing itself, comprehending all different branches of life's activities from Arts to Agriculture. Now it has come to a period, when we are fully aware of the absolute necessity of widening, across all barriers, the human sympathies of our students, – thus leading them to the fulfilment of their Education. This stage we have reached, as I have said, not through planning out my system, but by an inner life-growth, in which the sub-conscious has ever been bursting up with the conscious plans.

Lately it has come to us, almost like a sudden discovery, that our Institution is to represent that creative force which is acting in the bosom of the present age; passing through repeated conflicts and reconciliations, failures and readjustments, while making for the realisation of the spiritual unity of human races.

I have often wished, for my own mission, the help of men like yourself, who not only have a vast comprehensive sympathy and imagination, but also a wide range of knowledge and critical acumen. It has been with a bewilderment of admiration, that I have so often followed the architectural immensity of your own vision. But at the same moment, I have had to acknowledge that it was beyond my power to make a practical use of the background of perspective which your vision provides us with. The temperamental characteristics of my own nature require the greatest part of my work to remain in the sub-soil obscurity of mind. All my activities have the character of 'play' in them, – they are more or less like writing poems, only in different media of expression. Your own schemes also, in a great measure, have the same element which strongly attracts me, but they have a different idiom, which I have not the power to use. You will understand from this, my dear friend, that though I have always enjoyed listening to you, when you formulate your ideas, and my mind [illegible] is the vastness of their unity, I cannot criticise them. I suppose they are being stored in my conscious memory waiting for living assimilation with my own thoughts.

Cordially yours

Rabindranath Tagore

Dear Tagore,

Yes, I feared that my technical plan of my Dept. of Sociology and Civic
would be too dry for you! All plans must be so: that is their mathematical
nature and limitation. But they express concrete foundations also, and for
City and University alike – the latter too in its spiritual and ideal
completeness, – not for knowledge only, but *for* Good, True and Beautiful
together; as the best mind have always seen, but as each age and civilization
has to express anew, and as you are trying! (And with unusual share of
success!)

So think of us technical workers and students as planning out the
foundations for your and other ideal Universities – and locating more
clearly – and more spaciously too, the gardens of the Muses upon this
sacred Hill.

It was thus an agreeable result to find, for instance, as I said at Jerusalem,
that the *Great* Hall I had to plan for the University there worked out into
the hexagon and interesting triangles[91] which are the symbol of Israel[92] (as
the crescent for Islam, or the cross for Christianity). This gave a new style
of dome – for all others are on square or octagon – and thus a new style in
architecture.

But this came not to me not at all as seeking to realise the Jewish symbol
for them, as my Zionist friends at first naturally thought. It was really
worked out sixteen years or more before, before I had ever heard of
Zionism – and as an ideal Temple for the Unity of Life; (usually the Jewish
Ideal!) yet thus strictly derived from synthetising, in graphic forms, my
general knowledge of Biology – (Environment functioning on Organism,
yet Organism mastering Environment) and of Sociology and Civics –

---

91 There is a hand sketch of a star here with intersecting triangles.
92 There is a sketch of a swastika-like symbol just after and above 'Israel'.

Place conditioning <u>People</u>, yet <u>People</u> re-conditioning <u>Place</u>
    (— working)   [re-illegible]
                                        [re-illegible]
           More{briefly}still=
              {simply}
          Life-dynamic{E f o : O f e   (= Bergson etc. where
                                                developed)

                      and
            – Social {Pl w pe : Pe w Pl}

Mathematics and Logic – Technics and Physics, Arts and Esthetics, (Biotechnics = Agriculture, Medicine, etc.) and Biology, Education and Psychology, Politics and Economics, Religion and Ethics, are thus <u>all in</u> tune, so many strings for the philosophic harp, as well as of the poet's lyre! (Hence they helped in planning these University Buildings).

But you may say I am off again into my world of theories; so stop bothering you with these!

But just read the accompanying short Bombay University circular, as the first published product of this technical looking Department Plan of mine! You will, I am convinced, feel it has some human interest, and I trust more or less agree that it is on the lines of progress you can approve. (The preface is by Harold Mann especially – but all now adopted by University Committee and circulated accordingly.)

The difference between us is that while I work out (the equivalents of) musical <u>notations</u>, the <u>prosody</u> of thought, you can make songs as well as poems! (Yet you know your musical notation, your verse-notation too.)
(Why not then notation for <u>thought</u>? Not impossible, though ideas occur without them!)[93]

                 Ever yours

                 P Geddes

---

[93] This paragraph is added to the left-hand margin.

University of Bombay
Deptt of Sociology and Civics letterhead
(emblem)

Department of Sociology and Civics,

Bombay,

10 November 1922

Dear Tagore,

(My son &) I have spent two active days at Santiniketan and Sherul, following on one with Mahalanobis beforehand, in which he explained to me as much of the situation as might be.

They are sending me survey plans on which I can work, and I shall hope to send you what suggestions, report and developed plans as I can – say, by new year vacation, or sooner, – work here may allow. *(sic)*

In the meantime pray write me anything you can as to the future developments which you have in mind, even though not realizable soon, or with present means, so that I may at any rate leave room for them. Above all, give me your ideas as to the <u>numbers</u> you expect to provide for, in Boys School, in Girls and Women Students Departments, in College of Art, College of Music (and Drama?), College of Agriculture, etc. For these are each and all real and promising beginnings, invaluably supplementing (and I trust in time stimulating) the existing University Departments and Faculties elsewhere, as of Law, Medicine, Engineering etc. What, too, are your expectations of numbers of students and of teachers in Modern Literature (Indian & European) in Classics Sanskrit, Pali etc. and Philosophy? Do you intend making these varied – *i.e.* including French and German (if not Italian) as well as English, and also Hindi etc. with Bengali ?

Again, are you to teach Latin and Greek as well as Sanskrit, Pali etc? What scale and scope do you intend to give to mathematics, physics and chemistry? And what to Geological Sciences? Do you admit Sociology and Civics within your scheme? (Tacitly of course they are evident; but what of a specific teacher?).

I am sending a copy of this letter to Mahalanobis as secretary and as you will be seeing him, you need not spend precious time in writing me; he will do this. But pray be considering these questions and others, and give me your ideas as clearly as you can – <u>boldly</u> for the future – (and trusting to my keeping confidence, as to anything you may not wish announced or promised). For as the essence of all planning is foresight, it is your vision and ideal which must guide the whole scheme. Have you written of this anywhere? If so, can I have it (in Translation if need be)?

The term "International University" suggests comparison with that of my old friends Otlet and Lafontaine in Brussels, who have also the warmest sympathy with you. Are you in possession of their publications of which I have here only imperfect samples? If so, it will save time if you can spare it me for a brief perusal afresh, for though I have been over their scheme, buildings etc. I have not yet seen it in operation. (It is essentially a greatly developed "<u>Summer School</u>", such as I ran for many years at Edinburgh, and found stimulating all round to teachers & students alike.)

You, however, aim more distinctly at all the year round work.

But you cannot compete with Universities on the great world scale – at least for many years to come (such as I have been planning at Jerusalem – on a scale surpassing Oxford & Cambridge, Harvard & Chicago).

Your Colleges as aforesaid, of Agriculture, Fine Arts and Music, Modern and Ancient Literature, etc. I take to be your main concern, leaving boys who wish to enter law, medicine, engineering etc. to go elsewhere; yet as for preparing these also, as school may do. Am I right in this?

This seems to me also an opportunity for drawing out the ideas and dreams of development of the various responsible collaborations you have gathered round you, (and of whose character and spirit, as well as technical qualifications I have a very high and deep impression, and so cannot but congratulate you accordingly). Thus what do your artists groups, scholar groups, agricultural group, scientific groups, feel that they could (1) best <u>immediately utilise?</u> – and (2) will <u>gradually and ultimately require?</u> Similarly as to provision for girls and women, so far as these requirements differ from those of men?

All these are large demands: but if I am to plan (of course as economically as may be, and) in such a way as to meet growing and future requirements, I cannot be too fully "<u>briefed</u>", or too speedily.

– With congratulations and good wishes, *great* hopes also, believe me always

Yours faithfully and cordially

P Geddes

Bolpur
20 December 1922[94]

My dear Geddes,

I have every reason to believe that it was a fact that Rabindranath Tagore's visit to America in the winter of 1920-1921 was spoilt owing to the suspicion having been created through the British Embassy and its agents that he was anti-British. I know he felt this most acutely and he is not likely to forget it; though it has not soured him as much as might have been expected.

The same utterly fatuous thing happened in Australia. I cabled to Melbourne University asking if they would receive him but the hint was given that Rabindranath Tagore was 'seditious'. So his visit was cancelled.

Yours very sincerely,

C.F. Andrews.

---

[94] This handwritten letter shares the same date with the letter written by Andrews to Tagore from Bombay, which must be a mistake, as the above letter is written from Shantiniketan, Bolpur. Tagore was in America from 28 October in 1920 till March 1921, when his reputation following his public protest against the Amritsar Massacre was at its low ebb. Dutta and Robinson, 1995, pp. 229-230.

Mount Potit,
Poddar Road,
Bombay,
20 December 1922.[95]

My dearest friend,

I have been having long and extremely interesting talks with Professor Geddes on three separate mornings, which I have given up for him; and I have got from him now all his principal ideas about our own development. He is very critical indeed about what we have done in the building, and he says we have made a mess of it to start with; but all the same he believes in us thoroughly and in our future, and is quite eager for his son Arthur to come to us for this summer, while Elmhirst is away in America. He is himself so keen about us, that he said to me yesterday morning, "If you were 51 instead of 68 and nearing 70 years of age, I would throw in my lot with you. – Um! – For I think your's the most hopeful thing – Um! that I've ever seen in India".

By the way, I cannot tell you what a fortunate thing it was, that I stayed behind after you went and at once went and saw him. He was terribly hurt, because you had not come again to have a talk, and thought it showed a lack of interest. But I was able to put that right and to make ample amends, and now he is tremendously keen on helping all he can. He is very sensitive, like all Celts, but also very affectionate.

About one other personal matter, before I forget it, he is tremendously anxious that we should find some common ground of fellowship with Sir J.C. Bose, and says that it is a thousand pities that two such obviously complementary works should stand so far apart. He knows Sir J.C. Bose's limitations, but all the same he holds strongly, that these should be overcome by patience and kindliness and a more intimate basis to be established between the two institutions. He says, it used to be the happiest

---

95 This letter to Tagore is a typed copy, so the date is clear. Yet Andrews' letter of the same date, but handwritten, has the same date, but is written in Bolpur. There is, obviously, a mistake. This letter should predate the one written from Bolpur, after Andrews' return to Bolpur (which is the nearest town to Shantiniketan), from Bombay.

moment in Bose's life when he received a letter, or sometimes even a poem from you, congratulating him on some new discovery he had made. Dr. Geddes suggests that we should try to get the help and advice of Basiswar Sen who is (so he believes) by far the best of Bose's pupils. He ought to come over and advise us on the science side, and we should not neglect that side as we are doing at present.

To turn to another point, Prof. Geddes profoundly disagrees with your theory, when you say that Europe is 'one in race'. He said to me, – "The fact is the Poet doesn't <u>know</u> the West – Um!" – He states that from the very first we have had our own aborigines in Europe and three radically different races to assimilate – the Nordic, the Alpino and the Mediterranean, – and we have never got over the radical difference between the North and South of Europe. Rome could not manage the amalgamation of North and South, of barbarian and Mediterranean, and broke up while trying it. The 16th Century saw the same splitting asunder with the Reformation. Modern Europe is finding the same unconquerable divisions between the Teuton and the Latin. He said that all European history worked itself out along that line of division, which was essentially racial. What had been Europe's good fortune was to have had (over most of its area) one religion hammering it into shape all through the middle ages, and it took a lot of hammering.

I pointed out, that this was not the same as the great distinction between the regional aboriginal and the white Aryan. He said, – "Even there, I am not so sure, – Um! – The differences were almost as radical – and then you must remember the Hun and the Slav – Um! And then again, Islam had had a great slice of Europe, over many centuries, introducing all kinds of strange races and making the Balkans into a shambles again and again. No! Europe has had her racial troubles through and through, but she has had a unity of religion, and of intellectual alertness". – What I felt, after his talk, was that you ought to take up (in the long lazy hot months which are coming) some great book like Hodgkin's "Europe and her invaders", and read about "The Barbarian Invasions". Geddes repeatedly said to me:- "The truth is, the Poet does not really <u>know</u> the West. He was talking too loosely and inaccurately".

Arthur and I are working out together Prof. Geddes' Proposals for the new residential quarters. Here my long hours with him and his son may have been of great immediate value. He wants the ground plan of the whole area, for verification, but thinks that the best place for the new block will be about where Rathi and I thought, namely near to Suren's bungalow, but

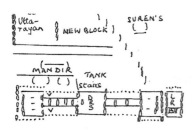

he suggests the <u>near</u> side of the road. He would have one block double storied, with a 'salon' and dining room, such as would hold 16 or 20 according as all were bachelors, or some were married. The design we considered would perhaps be roughly thus in its ground plan.

In this, the two ends might be for married people, up and down stairs; the middle might be for dining room and salon stairs. The other rooms up and down stairs for bachelors. But I am having a final talk over things with Arthur Geddes tomorrow and he may suggest some changes. I will keep this letter open till then. In the plan I have drawn, there might be a small bathroom for each room taking up a portion of the veranda. Geddes is keen on a double storey. He has said to me again and again, – "Pay your architect well and let him be a thoroughly sound and safe constructor: it will pay a hundred times over to get a very good man."

Geddes has with him here, in Bombay, a Parsee who is a born genius (so Geddes believes) in acting and dramatic work. His name is Khambatta and he wants him to join us and he thinks that he can persuade him to do so. I shall see him before leaving. He should be employed at once in working out and planning an open air theatre both at Santiniketan and at Surul. I am going to see Khambatta and I have hopes of him from what Geddes has said. I will let you know later.

Furthermore, Geddes is exceedingly keen on keeping our tank where it is, but spending money wisely in covering the bottom in the 'Dry Season' with hard clay as the foundation, which becomes brick-like and will not let water go through. He feels certain that we could get a good supply of water. I pointed out our difficulty namely that the ground slopes away from the tank and therefore only a slight amount of the surface water gets into it. Geddes urged however that the tank of water in that place, (if all the borders were well kept and a path round were made) would be one of the most pleasing features of the Asram; and even if we could not fill the whole, we ought to fill a part at least with water, and we ought to keep the remainder of the mound, – possibly with a view to an open air Theatre. He fully agreed with the idea of the open Mandir, with double columns. He liked very much indeed the old tiled roof. That should on no account should be destroyed. His strongest criticism of all was about the present kitchen building. He pointed out, how utterly unworthy it was, and how little could be done to make it worthy. He has promised me suggestions on this head. He greatly disliked the ugly front wall of the workshop compound, and wanted all that part revising and in part rebuilding but, he said, we must be very careful indeed to check our passion for re-building, because it was apt to take possession of one, and then it became 'biologically unhealthy'.

I want to tell you the good news about the students here. They are utterly with you; and when you come here next time, on your way to Europe or elsewhere, they will give you the best reception you have had anywhere in India. Only think of this one fact, that the magic of your name brought over a thousand together on Monday. After the College was closed, and when attendance was entirely voluntary, and again yesterday an equal number came together at 4.30 in the afternoon, which is their only time for games! We could not get the Excelsior Theatre at any other time, and so it had to be arranged at this most objectionable hours! On both occasions they passed resolutions declaring their support. They have also promised, after Christmas, when I come again to have a student's contribution. Meanwhile they are forming committees in each College to collect annual members, and to form a Visva-Bharati Samaj. I could not hurry on things further now because the Christmas holidays are near and there have been an extraordinary number of distractions; but I can safely say now that the students here are with you heart and soul. One of them said to me, "Tell Gurudev we quite understood that he could not come round to all the Colleges, and we could not expect him to do so. But when he does come, he will have such a reception as even his Calcutta students have never given him! We are all reading his works."

At the students' meeting, this afternoon, Miss Vlaun from Jerusalem came forward afterwards, to my great delight. She has landed in India at last after many difficulties and trials. She is quite the type we need, in every way, and she has gone over mountains of difficulties in order to come to Santiniketan. Her courage and determination are wonderful, and she is

78

very quiet and able to put up with every hardship; and she is also a vegetarian and a follower of Tolstoy. But she has not yet got her full passport for India, and I must at once do all I can at Delhi, (where fortunately I am going tomorrow), or else she may be sent back again. All she has got are her Turkish papers with the British Consul's visa: she is being kept here in Bombay under supervision. I am going down this morning to see after it all. How fortunate it is I was here for her: otherwise she would have had very little chance indeed.

I want to tell you one thing, that has been quite constantly in my mind. You know I have always told you, that I have felt you have never done justice to the Old Testament and its development. What is on my mind is, that we must have a true scholar, a Hebruist, with a modern mind, who can teach Hebrew and lecture on the Hebrew Prophets in Santiniketan, not a Christian, but a Jew. I talked this over with Miss Vlaun, and she tells me she knows the very person who may even be ready to come out to us Dr. Klause, – because he is sharing already our ideals and is himself as a scholar making investigations as to the relations of India with the Jewish people from the earliest days. If he can come, we shall get the Calcutta and Bombay Jews to support him.

We must not forget that India opened her doors hospitably to the Jews from a very early date and they have settled in India, – not in as large numbers as the Parsees, but still in an appreciable manner. They also form, from the deeper religious point of view, the key to very much that happened in Western Asia. And one of the great fields of history, still unexplored, is the relation of India (with its central geographical position) to Western Asia. All that you have studied about ancient Persia will show you how vast is the field of discovery in this direction. It will link India with Egypt also, when all the tangled tale is unravelled.

I cannot yet say very much about the final collections in Bombay, – what we can hope, – but I have been altogether convinced by this week's experience, that they cannot be gathered in just now. You cannot understand what pressure has been brought from every side of Government, in order to make a success of the Red Cross Fete, and thus show their strength against N.C.O., which boycotted it. The result has been, that everyone has been canvassed till they are sick of it. Also Christmas holiday time, in Bombay, is a buying and a holiday time and people don't like to give large sums just before such a holiday. Everyone urges that things will be far better in January, and that it will not be the case that the enthusiasm over your visit will have died away. I am fully inclined to accept this diagnosis and to come and appeal later, after literature has been well circulated and the ideas about Visva-Bharati themselves are better known. The pamphlet, which is now published and is going round, will, I am sure, be of great service.

Today I have felt something of the old energy I had come back to me. – The worst of the time I have been through has been, that every single thing has been a great burden. One wakes up, tired, in the morning and forces oneself to go through the day, and goes to bed, tired, – only to get up tired again. You have known this so well yourself during these past months, for I have seen it in you, – I have a very great dread of those three days in Lahore of 'Railway Federation' meetings; but as it is absolutely the only way of materially helping over a million people directly, and many more indirectly, (for the Railways of India are the key to the whole industrial problem) I could not possibly see my way to get out of it; and it has had the one advantage of bringing me up to the Punjab, where I can really tackle Sultan Singh and others about Visva-Bharati itself. I have been wishing for long to do this; for I am certain that he ought to take the lead among the Jain community. And it is fortunate in this, that I shall be able to see Rudra again, about whom I have been getting more and more anxious. But I cannot tell you in words how my mind and body alike are crying out for rest!

With my very dearest love

Charlie. [Andrews]

I have seen the Government here about Miss Vlaun; they have wired to Bengal Government. I have wired also suggesting that we at Santiniketan give our guarantee about her bona fide character.

P.S. I have had a very long talk with Irani and as it was an extremely important one I have opened this letter to add to it. He fully agrees with me that you have done quite right concerning the Ratan Tata Trust and he is delighted that we have not asked for more at once. But he and Justice Mulla also hope very much that he will give a private donation which will materially help us. There is no trouble whatsoever about the Parsees. You have won their hearts and the rest will follow. I am seeing Irani again today and we shall interview another of his clients. But he is quite certain, that the time to make a full collection is not <u>now</u>, when the Red Cross *Fete* and Christmas are in the way, but during the last part of January, – I put before him the possibility of the first part of January, but he said at once and decidedly: 'No'. When I saw Narottam and the Hindus, they also said the same thing; but they have promised me to do their utmost if I come for the latter half of January. So I must go direct to the South from Ahmedabad and not stay in Bombay at all.

Then, there is one further extremely important point. Irani says (and I fully agree with him) that you must spare Morris for that period, and that he must come a very few days before my return. He suggests that Morris should come on Jan 15th and I should come on Jan 20th. There are a hundred details that Morris can do easily, as he knows Bombay so well, while it is impossible for me and it would only waste my time. Mrs. Petit fully agrees with this plan of operations, and while she wants to help very much indeed, it would very clearly have been a great burden to her to have tried to help us earlier in January just after her husband's return and after the Red Cross Fete which has quite worn her out. Again, it will be much the best for the students; for they will have just settled down after the Christmas holidays which go on till Jan 7th and they will be ready for a fresh effort.

I feel much happier after this long talk and I can see that we shall reach the Hindu Community best through those who really love us – through Ambalal, through young Mr. Rao, and above all through Irani himself who has nearly all his client Hindus. As his special work among them is challenging 'Income tax assessments' in Court, they are obliged to reveal to him, their solicitor, their true income; and he has now placed our Santiniketan in the forefront of the charitable institutions which he asks them to support. He believes that we can safely rely on quite a steady income in this manner.

Mrs. Petit was delighted with your letter and Hillabhai too. You have won their hearts quite easily and they were easy for you, with all your wealth of love and affection, to win; for they respond like flowers to sunlight. – It has been a great happiness to Mrs. Petit to have had me here during these days of the Red Cross Fete, when she has been quite tired out, for as she told me I am now one of her family who can help her and not a visitor at all. I only wish I could have done more for her; but it was sympathy and understanding that she chiefly needed, and I could give her these.

Please give my love to Morichi and let him have all the news, and spare him from January 15th.

Just one word more. You cannot realise what great happiness you gave to all this household by your visit. It has been a blessing, not only to Mrs. Petit herself, but to all the children. Dinshaw is working hard for us in his College, and all of them speak about you with reverence and affection. This gift of blessing, which you have given to her children, – just at this difficult time of their life, – has touched Mrs. Petit most of all. You have won all their hearts.

Dear Geddes,

Andrews has told me all the trouble you are taking over us and of your hope for the institution. Elmhirst tells us that you are quite keen on Arthur coming here. It would be delightful to have him here to advise us on the carrying out of your schemes which we will gladly follow within the limit of our resources. I see no reason at all why he should not keep his health at Surul. Miss Green has promised to try and act as a mother to him. She has made a different man of Elmhirst and I think you could trust her to guard him from malaria. Besides this the malaria season does not get into full swing until July. With his help Surul could be malaria-proof within three months. We can offer him Rs. 150/- per month for his expenses. Lodging is free, board will come to about Rs. 30-40, and servant Rs. 30-40.

Your idea of the graphic representation of human life and mind, the cycle of their activities and varied manifestations has strongly captured my mind. I wish we could make a place for it in our institution. It is not in our power to collect at once all the materials necessary for it, but we can make a start if we have an efficient guidance. Will Arthur be able to help us if it becomes possible for him to come? I hope some day some of your students may take up this work here. While I was in Bombay I was so fatigued and my mind distracted with work for which I have no aptitude that I could not see you as often as I wished. I am waiting for Andrews to come when I shall know something about the interviews he had with you.

Yours truly

Rabindranath Tagore

as at c/o Ambalal[96]
Shahibag
Ahmedabad
1923[97]

My dear Geddes,

I have been having many talks over the new residential quarters with your son. I think I have convinced him that every possible veranda space should be given and the inner room made comparatively small not vice versa. The one essential to remember with residence in Bolpur is that every wind that blows is a blessing and you cannot have too much of it. It is not like the Punjab when you have to shut up all day long. My own idea would be a series of rooms with a 10 foot veranda on either side and a 10'—15' space for the room itself. The bathroom might be quite small in the course of the East Veranda. The rooms should be broad wise rather than length wise with plenty of door and window spacing. I would suggest that the ground plan be something like this as this would break the appearance of a barrack like building. I am working it out with your son Arthur but I thought you would like to know of our conception.

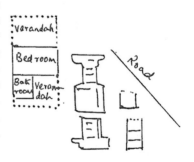

I believe the mound by the side of the tank will have to come into use in the open air Theatre.

Yours very sincerely

C.F. Andrews

[96] On the top, before the address, there is a handwritten note by Geddes saying, 'Santiniketan. (abbreviated as 'Sant.n.') – <u>Andrews</u>.'
[97] This letter is not dated. Since it indicates Andrews having had some planning sessions with Arthur, it could have been during the period Arthur Geddes spent at Shantiniketan. The letter, written in Ahmedabad, could be composed on one of Andrews' many visits to the Mahatma, whose Ashram was close to the city.

Dear Professor Geddes,

The poet has handed to me your letter of Jan 10th and I feel guilty for not having written in answer to your previous one. I am trying to save my brain from bursting before March! And I'm almost on the verge of disaster but think I can hold out till then. These lectures in Calcutta take it all out of me mentally, though physically I'm fit enough.

Quite a number of villages round us have their old Jatra[98] parties which act folk plays etc. and we are doing our best to stimulate and encourage them. Our theatre will be of great service there, but at the moment we haven't funds to finish digging the tank.

So the poet says by all means let them come and survey the field. As to the rest, the wretched Kanungo, (Government surveyor) who drew our plan, which rightly disgusted you, is back – but I see no prospect yet of our getting another. Rathi Tagore is trying to get what pictures he can from the school and I believe has a surveyor at work.

Between[99] ourselves I am afraid delay is inevitable, though I hate to say it, and I am simply trying to prepare the ground so that Arthur can give the necessary guidance when he comes. I do hope he can come here before the end of February, and I'm sure you need have little fear for him so long as he is cooked for and mothered by Mrs. Green. I'd have been in a lunatic asylum long ago if it had not been for her.

---

[98] *Jatras* belong to the folk theatre tradition of Bengal, performed on an open stage with the audience sitting all round it. The plays are usually based on the stories from the Indian epics, the *Ramayana* and the *Mahabharata* and Hindu mythology. Sometimes popular stories are used and even historical and topical themes. Villages have their own Jatra group with its equipment and the actors are amateurs from amongst the village population. There are also some itinerant professional groups. The plays are performed on makeshift stages in temporary tents and whole villages turn out to witness performances which can last through the night.

[99] This reads like an abbreviation of 'Between', though the fountain pen strokes do make it more of a guess than a certainty.

Andrews is hopeless, off to the flood areas and likely to be engrossed in Relief for some time to come. My only hope here now is in Suren Tagore[100] who though unsuccessful in business has a head on him and real understanding of the practical means for carrying out the poet's schemes. Andrews means well and is a man of good heart, but I cannot see that he comprehends much of what the poet is really aiming at and politics, strike and reliefs occupy the balls of his energy, necessary no doubt, but in the end the energy invested hardly bears any true interest?

I've just got my camera working and am getting all the pictures I can.

I'm worried too over funds for my own place here, and I'm investing rather heavily in a cinema film to carry with me via China to America, giving this end of the poet's work.

I expect to be in Ithaca NY about the end of June, so if you are in U.S.A. write me c/o The Telluride (sic) Association Ithaca New York (to await arrival)

The poet says he has written regarding Arthur – did he make condition of pay, board etc. plain or what is to be the arrangement, – let's have it clear, – for they are awfully casual in these matters here.

As to the Surul tank – lease is impossible, but all the leaders in the village have promised to carry out a full programme which I have sketched, and through Miss G's[101] work the big division has been healed and we hope for united action.

I feel guilty *somehow* that I haven't properly backed up your end of the work, but I know you'll realise how almost impossible it is to get things to move here, – delay, delay delay, we'll see, – tomorrow, and so forth and even the best labour is inefficient.

However, dairy, weaving and tannery schemes are coming along.

---

[100] The pen strokes read like 'Suren Tagore' and not 'Kar'. We know that Suren Kar, the architect, did help in the designing and implementation of many of the buildings at Shantiniketan and that Suren Tagore, Tagore's nephew, was a literary figure in his own right.
[101] Probably 'Green's'?

Lord Lytton lunched with the poet and myself here two days ago and was apparently delighted. He promised every support.

Yours very sincerely,

L.K. Elmhirst

I sail *in* March![102]

Dear Geddes,

Your letter came to me at the auspicious moment when the Governor of Bengal with his retinue came to visit the Ashram. I had just time to read your letter hastily and then lost it. I am sure I shall find it some day when it is too late. You may ask your American friends to come to us. We shall try to give them the informations they seek and take them round to Surul. I am trying to stage a play of mine in Calcutta to raise some money for the flood affected parts of Bengal. If our visitors have time they may have chance to witness it and get some idea of our modern play acting.

I am afraid there will be some delay in Andrew's starting for Bombay owing to his mission for the suffering people of Bengal. I hope he will be able to meet you sometime in February and have a discussion about our building plan and other things.

We are looking forward to Arthur's coming to us,

Yours

Rabindranath Tagore

---

[102] And in March we do find Arthur writing to his father from Shantiniketan.

Santiniketan P.O.
District Birbhum
Bengal
21 January 1923[103]

Dear Professor Geddes,

I am in receipt of your letter and have made enquiries about your plans. I find that for some time they were held up because no competent surveyor could be found to complete the details. Now however Rathi Babu assures me that they are in hand and ought to be finished within a few days. They will be sent to you as soon as they are completed.

I have spoken to the Poet about your suggestion as to help in U.S.A. and he will talk it over with Elmhirst who is starting for America via China and Japan at the beginning of March.

With kind regards

Yours very sincerely

W.W. Pearson

---

[103] The letter does not have the year on it. Elmhirst's letter of 29 May 1923 to Geddes, confirms the details mentioned in Pearson's letter, which suggests that it was written around the same time.

VISVA-BHARATI
(THE SANTINIKETAN UNIVERSITY)
[Seal]

Pratisthata-Acharya
(Founder President)
Rabindranath Tagore

[Seal]

Regd. Office:
Santiniketan
Bengal, India

Calcutta Office:
210 Cornwallis St.
26 January 1923

Dear Prof. Geddes,

Your plan is in an active state of preparation now. Rathi Babu is hoping to be able to send it to you within a few days. We are very badly in need of advice.

I am glad Arthur is coming to stay at Bolpur for some time. I am sure he will like it very much.

I am very busy just at present. But I shall let you have a few points of my own about future development at the time of sending you the plan.

With kind regards,

Yours sincerely,

P. C. Mahalanobis

P.S. I am writing to the Poet about your kind offer to help us in U.S.A. I think it will be best if we formally authorise you (by means of a resolution by the Governing Body) to represent us there during your coming tour.

PCM

Dear Geddes,

I am sure Mr. Khambatta can be of very great use to us. But I wonder how can we secure his services. My efforts at raising funds in Bombay have hardly been successful. Now I am arranging to go to Sind for the same purpose, possibly with the similar result in prospect. I am very anxious to realise enough money to be able to ask Dr. Brajendranath Seal to take his seat in our University. Our arts and crafts department, our village work organisation are showing signs of life. We want some one who can infuse life into the academic branch of our work and I believe Dr. Seal can do it. But I think we shall have to wait.

If it is possible for Mr. Khambatta to come and see this place I shall be glad to have a talk with him. There is some chance of my visiting Bombay for a day or two on my way to Karachi – possibly in the second week of March. In that case I shall arrange a meeting with him in Bombay.

Yours

Rabindranath Tagore

University of Bombay
[Seal]

University of Bombay
Department of Sociology and Civics
Royal Institute of Science
Bombay.
26 February 1923.

Dear Mahalanobis (Collaborator to Tagore)[104]

The plan has at length arrived – yesterday afternoon, as I was leaving for excursion with students, so will be opened to-morrow. I trust it may be found all right for working on.

But alas, <u>there is now no time</u> for this. When it was promised me by all concerned in the beginning of November, and "<u>in a few days</u>" – "<u>and without fail</u>" – I was at a rare period of freedom for it. Also I had my mind full of clear mental photographs of Shantiniketan, with which I was ready and free to work, (even without the concrete photographs for which I asked, and which were also promised me with the same amiable assurance, but which also never arrived and – (presumably) – forgotten.

Still I might recall my memories, and work now. But last November I was then free of other plannings, and until Xmas – a very rare opportunity for work on your problems, and on which I was then fresh, as well as keen.

But I had in the Xmas vacation (of less than a fortnight to go) *(sic)* and tackle (1) the Lucknow Zoo, and also the Osmania University at Hyderabad each, and especially the latter, on large scale and needing much work. They thus pledged me to my remaining free time – (after term here closes 10th. to sailing for home and U.S.A. on 31st.)

Next came in the demand for criticism of Bombay City Improvements: each of the three is largest of its kind in the cities of the world at present – and the <u>worst</u> in execution with corresponding urgency.

---

[104] The parenthesis is added by hand to a typed letter.

Next this University has gone into eruption – and I have its future planning on my hands – with regular meetings of Committee concerned accordingly.

Finally, the new Non-Co-Operative University College at Ahmedabad. Again with plans, visits from Principal and active correspondence.

And now the electricians are wiring in this department – with the confusion accordingly. And I have ten days to wind up my (thus disordered) exhibition, and do what I can to plans of all preceding, before leaving Bombay for Lucknow and Hyderabad, before sailing.

So instead of having your plans ready, and your case clear to plead in America as I hoped last November I have just nothing – save disappointments all around. For, while the poet made a fairly long visit to Bombay and I met him at dinner one evening and he gave a look at Exhibition, one morning, the promised business talk never came off. While Mr. Andrews at length managed to get time for one Hostel, which was planned accordingly.

But such things are taken more seriously by all other clients, in my nine years experience in India; so rarely with my disappointment like this. Thus, the Principal of Osmania and his engineer worked with me all day and every day on ground during week there, and then they came here for a week, all day and every day again. With result that we know where we are each working up in correspondence towards another fortnight together, – again on the site in discussion point by point – "hammer and tongs".

Somewhat similarly now with the Principal at Ahmedabad.

But no one in Shantiniketan, or of it, seems yet to realise that this is how any large planning gets properly done, and that very active cooperation and discussion is necessary between client and planner – as with patient and doctor, with customer and tailor.

Do not therefore mistake this letter for a mere grumble. It is first the needed explanation of why, despite all hopes and ardent goodwill – and even a good deal of thought – I am now quite unable to work on this plan since too late delivered; but shall have to send it back to my son at Sherul, with such notes – too brief and few, as I can find time for – so that he may be doing what he can this summer, in contact with all concerned, a very important matter. And I shall be able to go over them with, and with any of your Committee who may come to Bombay – from next November (10th. onwards). But I can't come to Shantiniketan till next Xmas and perhaps not even then.

I shall also do my best to go over what he can send me to U.S.A. meantime – but that is no easy matter. With New York City survey more or less in hand, and University visits all over.

The promised briefing for my U.S.A. visit has also not arrived; but even now I shall do what little I can there, if I am still to get it before sailing. (I might even make some progress with planning in such quiet time as may be on voyage.)

So far then the needed explanation of the now inevitable and now disappointingly longer delays on my part to get out an alternative Plans and a Report. However we'll surely manage next winter, instead of this one – (if the poet, and Andrews and you can spare any time.)

The French proverb – "clear understanding makes good friends"[105] is here necessary: hence the letter.

And for similar reasons, I have lately written to Mr. Andrews putting to him with similarly painful candour, what I have learned here and elsewhere from others, and often less friendly than I – which largely at least explains the poet's, his and your general disappointment as to deficient support of scheme in India and beyond. Ask him to show it you. For I believe his situation can be relieved, and public support increasingly obtained. I hope to talk over with Andrews, if and when he comes.[106]

---

[105] The end of the quote is not indicated in the original, so it has been added where one surmises, the proverb ends.
[106] The copy of the letter on which this is based, is not finished or signed, but it is clearly from P. Geddes.

University of Bombay
[Seal]

28 February 1923

Dear Arthur,

Very glad to hear you have got on so well, and alike with Elmhirst and with seeing Poet's play, and also Lewisolms *(sic)*, Boshi, and I trust also Jo[107]? and Miss Addams? Also Iyengar? And Dr. Bentley (This chief) Jo <u>is</u> <u>[illegible][108] on malaria</u> at Belur Math, which plays havoc with the monks: so may stir them up to parallel action with yours, getting fish into Tanks and so on; and thus all reacts to strengthen Iyengar's hands, and Faculty too.

(You need not fear one bit but that Boshi and Co, as also Prof. Nag, (Chief in Bose's absence) will teach you, and any amount: only naturally he is down at present. I'll write to Bose also on your behalf, a month from now, when you have your programme clearer.)

Very attractive programme! Every point excellent! Yes. <u>C</u> *(sic)* – herewith, you have the gradual development of planning for Santiniketan – which I can't go into, beyond another day or so, over general questions, with answers here: we'll then compare notes when we meet in autumn – and of course you'll tell me of developments when writing me week by week, as I hope you'll do – like a good son, who keeps up contacts with his prodigal father, on his wanderings!

Of course see that they soon give you tracings, (or lend you originals) of the plans sent me.

I have been very firm with Andrews regarding the 5 blots of bad wasteful and pretentious architecture, and I tell him that I'll wash hands of whole thing if this is to go on! He quite agrees – but explains poet's desire to give freedom – also poet's son and artist are great friends, and latter has

---

[107] Possibly 'Jo'.
[108] Possibly 'keen'.

94

hypnotised former – for son built Nanda Lal Bose's building which is not bad, but was seduced later by the artist – a good painter, says Andrews. You have thus a delicate situation to handle; but you have time.

Andrews likes ideas of general University development and of making public understand Santiniketan as no mere "one man show" – but as developed Colleges – Agriculture, Arts, Medicine, Literature etc. which can and will go on, developed independently, and with him also understood as Prof. *of Agricultural* Economy, and as antidote to Political Economy (middle class mythology of Mammon and machine)[109] – (a good definition to rub into people!)

Then too I put to him the idea of all these new Universities as forming a new group of more synthetic and social character than heretofore, in fact increasingly breaking with the cramshops of the past and its village service etc. to lead this series of new groupings too and thus giving a lead for those as such who desire change. Osmania for Arabic, for Vernaculars, for [illegible] of Islam and so on. I am trying him too with the Tower. Just as Santiniketan will have intellectual distinction at highest (Einstein and Co) so it is for Santiniketan with its poetic leadership (piper to play before Moses) and its village service etc. to lead this series of new groupings too.[110]

---

[109] In a similar vein, Tagore says, 'Those who are familiar with the Hindu Pantheon know that in our mythology there is a demi-god named Kuvera, similar in character to Mammon. He represents the multiplication of money whose motive is greed… He is the genius of property that knows no moral responsibility.' *The Visva-Bharati Quarterly*, Vol II, No. 3, October, 1924 (Bengali: Kartic 1331), p. 220.

[110] The end of this letter is missing.

I do hope you met the Poet.

Dear Daddy,

Your notes sent by G.G.A. have come. Very glad to look over them; I know they will be very suggestive. My village investigation has not yet begun; too many problems of planning etc. at which I seem to be of some use, and am in some demand, at Santiniketan and here, (Sriniketan; or "Surul Khoti"). I realise that I was a little rash, perhaps, in saying that there would be no more of the fanciful architecture of Suren Kar, – Rathi Tagore's artist confederate, – since Rathi's (the Poet's son's) house is still to build, while the foundations are laid, and the plan, therefore, is fixed. Still, Rathi is making a model, and Vowan Rao (the new young architect) will redraw the elevation, with perspective, and probably make quite a nice job. They <u>are</u> naive here: Rathi said "let's have nothing built without having a plan first"! Vowan Rao (Architect) is keen to meet you and nearly asked permission to go to Lucknow to talk over things with you. However he's very busy, and finally decided he'd better stay.

As well as planning we're trying to clear the place up, – move those broken down carts, tidy away the wrecks, the heaps, the middens, the mosquito holes and drains and actually fix up camp latrines. "Gandhi Day" – in memory of a sort of fiery visit here 8 years ago of Mahatmaji's, was celebrated on Saturday by a holiday, all the servants being relieved of their duties by volunteer cooks, etc., while Pearson, though keeping tactfully in the background as a mere labourer, managed to get up a corps of cleaners, which I joined, to see who would work and also for fun). They worked well for an hour or two, and got quite keen. This had its effect in suggesting a bigger clean-up from H.Q., and hastening its execution. Someone noticed there were hardly any Bengalis among the cleaning corps, mostly W. India, etc!

I wish you could draw your salary for lecturing here, instead of Bombay for now you're getting the University and city too, underway there. Your ideas would be lapped up here and with the chance of execution and experiment in the country and cloister that the poor Bombay L.L.B.s lack, though they've good intentions, poor fellows. I realise how welcome you'd be from the keen way they took my talks on P.W.F.[111] my 2nd last night, – both teachers and students at Santiniketan. It seemed relevant to them, with their rural and "international ideal" aims.

It is a pity these two places – Santiniketan and Sriniketan in Surul Khoti are so far apart, but it can't be helped, and on the whole there is some unity and good feeling between the two.

My teaching here consists of 2 nature study double-periods an hour and a half each, per week, 2 library evenings, at first discussion on plans, etc. maps, ways of tackling our surveys of nature and man. The students of Sriniketan are just +10 boys who came down here from Santiniketan school a year ago, but they're developing into manly fellows varying very much. They're gradually taking charge of special jobs – dairy, tannery, weaving, scouting, and each has his garden-plot, and most have chickens. The staff have complete charge of the above, one whose special ally I hope to be is a wonderful village worker, – pulling the people together in his gentle way with great success, – Kali Babu, by name.

With love to you, and to Norah when you can send this on.[112]

---

[111] P.W.F. : *Place, Work, Folk.*
[112] Though the signature is not on the copy of this hand-written letter, it is obviously from Arthur Geddes to his father.

My dear Daddy,

In our busy days since we parted we've had little time for other than letters of journal sort, a diary. I have, before you go, to look back on our 16 months together, and our winter to come, and who knows what after that? I look back with pleasure to our work for a year past. In Patiala especially I was finding my feet, and in Sociology too my old feeling and belief that your thought was what was needed for re-interpretation has been confirmed. What are you going to tell us about next winter? Give us warning some months before and then we can think things out beforehand and be ready with questions in our heads, and tuned for it; so that I trust you may find us not so stale, more responsive or suggestive than heretofore. And when you come back, I hope you'll find me better equipped both as student disciple and assistant, and as son too.

I've been asking myself again how I can train for effective co-operation whether nearer, or further, as here, and certainly this Santiniketan work seems excellent in every way, all round the Life Diagram, as seldom possible, and never quite before to me.

In a way I'm glad Elmhirst is away for it gives me more responsibility and intellectual freedom. Yet I feel him a future ally in life such as I've seldom met, or not yet at all, and a friend lost through his departure. Still in a way we're making a friendship by experience, – "filiated", if not "common", experience, in the usual sense. I'm anxious that he should feel I have been loyal to his aim in execution as well as intention, while not rigidly sticking to his suggestions by any means. There is nothing more essential than that work should be carried on with full regards for past attainment, so that this shall not be lost, and due regard for past plan. Above all in India and in this ramshackle institution. 'Stunts' are excellent in their way, but only if related to the whole and understood as such.

I now hear from Vowan Rao (Architect) has sent the photos to you. The survey of this place Sriniketan is still held up, – (the overseer is not very efficient) and so I'll send sketch plan for [illegible] Staff Quarters.

Vol I Leplay has just come. It looks much more readable than Comte! (also better print.)

I'll probably have more time for Village and survey work, and general reading etc. by April 1st. Brorby *(sic)* and Waring are coming then (the Americans who called at Bombay in Feb.) leaving 3 weeks later!

Our latest stunt is a "Masque of the Desert" – <u>Act I</u>. The Forest Hunter becoming Agriculturist – Vedic Age etc. II This breaking down through deforestation, drought, famine – the "Spirit of the Desert" advances pushing all before him. III The Desert pushed back by the Sriniketan boys. They dig a channel for Water, who dances along it, awakening "Earth", who throws off her sackcloth and appears in green. General rejoicing!

We may sketch out Act I on Saturday. This is the best I can do for Khambatta, – make him wanted.

I drew out yours and Frank's[113] Palestine diagram, – The Olive terraces drying up etc. then asked the students of the Nature Study Class (Srineketan) to draw out this for our bit of country, which 2 or 3 did very well and the others then caught on I think, or followed.[114]

---

[113] This is probably a reference to Frank Mears, the architect son-in-law of Geddes, who collaborated with Geddes in the planning of the International (Hebrew) University at Jerusalem.

[114] The end of this letter is missing.

Montpellier 30.4.4 *(sic)* but from
17 May to 17 June 1923
c/o Dr. Jucot La Colline,
Territet Switzerland

Dear Arthur,

Herewith a letter to read, close, and post to Andrews which needs no explanation. Except perhaps that the points I'd wish to rub in, after those of Indore Report, would be *e.g.*

(1) <u>Tower continued</u> as planning the Report to City and University Collection Collaboration (of which you might get a copy from Registrar University Bombay to pass around? as indeed of Dr. Mann's Report also).

(2) NS and my Civilisation Courses By – uniting Humanities and Geotechnics in their historic development and present condition.

(3) Medical Village, under discussion I am just raising here, as with Brook at Edinburgh.

(4) Zoo (mainly on bank next Tank) and Botanical Garden, (diffused over the place as at Dundee).

(5) Regional Survey (6) Art in Environment and so on.

Do try to get them to do something, begin something, to show Poet when he returns. What of Temple clearance of old iron? What of Tank and Zoo? And so on: go over your notes and ground.

Art: More and more I meditate the idea of <u>Art</u> as aroused anew by Civic and Regional Progress, to whole environment, and thus reissue from its last tiny retreat, of picture frame, into the widening world.

This place, cold and grey and colourless, dull, is the very expression of the cold intellectualism of France from Descartes and earlier to modern

University, to political abstractions, etc. etc. The revival of Art and that of Civics etc., all in a piece with the returning philosophy of Life and escape from post mortem abstractions accordingly. It is the absent mind which creates, and tolerates, and maintains the ugliness of the modern age – in its deadly (f)utilitarianism.

Much pleased to re-read Demolin's? "Comment la Route? Crée le Type Social" and "Les Français du Aujourdhui?". I am asking Mme Colin (now bookseller) to send you them. Pray read, mark, digest, and apply. These will I am sure help you to realise the interactions of P.W.F. etc. more concretely of also of world than I have ever taught them.[illegible] I wish we had such books in English!

You will I trust be pleased with my Medical Village – Epidauras/os of Montpellier! on the near Garrigne, with panorama of City and against Mediterranean. Just possible that they may wake up to it!

Mr. Houch, Alasdair's teacher of Cello was playing with Suzanne today, a Bach Sonata, and spoke very warmly of him, and also of his lessons to you. It would be nice if you would write Suzanne (or Tante Jeanne, as you prefer) to thank them for their hospitality to me, and say how pleased I am to go somewhere to tea almost daily. Also sympathies to poor Dr. Bousquet, still very ill – lying out in garden by day, but always suffering.

Wonderful School across this road from Pension – Abbé [illegible] Orphanage. Big buildings, very fine modern 13th Century Gothic church, as modern architecture goes, and better reproduction of stained windows of that time than I've seen before: really aflame in sunshine. Children sing and spiritually. Big garden, ready to work and sell plants to public – landscape proper, Ecole Professionnelle! And a Zoo, of birds anyway, very free – in full Franciscan tradition, (though I don't know if Abbé preaches to them!) All these points in advance of schools seen before.

What of a bit of Pagoda Aviary for Santineketan? It could be extended by degrees, and would give character to place, with minimum cost! Help to bring buildings together etc.

Do keep in mind the <u>Theatre-Hall and Outlook Tower!</u> It is a pity the ground falls towards the long main perspective it should close, but after all not too badly. And they need one such large building.

You might give young Tagore etc. an idea of my letter to Andrews, and of its points, not detailed to Andrews, but as named on p.i.

Do you find Nanda Lal Bose with any interest out of doors in aspects of building etc. or other painters?

How do you get on with that shocking Amateur Architect of Art School? Is he now restrained? Have you disillusioned Tagore at all – or is he still pleased? Has the architect who there done anything and what?[115]

---

[115] The copy of this handwritten letter does not include the conclusion or Geddes' signature as 'Daddy'. There is an attached sheet of jottings under 'CFA', which, by its very nature – of being notes with various abbreviations, is not very clear. There is mention of the Indore Report, of J.C.B. (Dr. Jagadish Chandra Bose), Tagore, Surul and the Central Hall.

Dear Tagore,

I hope you are having a better rest now after your rounds and before new year?

Here I am in compulsory rest of nursing-home: but waste no pity, a good past-time; and now being fed up for a few days at [illegible] or [illegible] before term. (Ailment not serious, stopped in time)

Dr. however (Carter, of Mesopotamian fame – first rate chap) says "Enough now of India, old chap: go home." – and I suppose I must obey, as now in 70th year.

Sorry however to leave India. We must get those plans clearer first! Can you do anything? *e.g.* its chapel-Temple relieved of its iron wall? Is Tank tidied up for its bank with trees, for part aviary[116] (we won't call it Zoo!) Above all, are you clear about the very real need of stopping the inroads of the Desert – and replanting it? The more I think of that, the more convinced I feel that that will be at once one of your great reconstructive and educative lessons – and in time a good investment for the University too. And to get [illegible] good stretch of that land, at its present minimum value, before you show its improvement, is so have prices raised against you *(sic)*, is but ordinary prudence.

Again, its boys' accommodation is too crowded, each new doubled space, with a little mobile-partition from his neighbour. And the dining room from a very dull and even untidy [illegible] ugly-aspect. Yet don't escape bad [illegible] at school! brutal frankness: it is [illegible][117]. Enough of this. I am asking Arthur, if he gets to Calcutta (on another job) at least, to

---

116 'Aviary' is a surmise, as Geddes has mentioned such a possibility elsewhere.
117 This letter is particularly smudged as the fountain pen used seems to have spilled over the written words, which accounts for the illegibility of not just words but phrases. The essence of the letter, is however, recoverable from the readable sections.

spend a day or so at Santiniketan, to refresh my notes and impressions together. He is at my "Zoo" at Lucknow, as I can't get away.

I shall not be going home till after March, so if you come again to Bombay pray let us have another talk. The important matters in University design are after all the <u>ideas</u>, and their <u>manifestation</u> – in no mere administrative way, but as vital and synthetic, in contrast to the present mechanical and analytic. What you – and of course so far justly – think of as "<u>science</u>", is for us of the biological and social sciences, mere analysis of the physical environment; for the most part, even that misunderstood and misapplied: civic, while unrelated to Life, and its science, these can but turn to death – wholesale in war, but produced and retailed in (so called) peace. Bergson is on a better way – but Arthur Thomson for biology, Branford for sociology are offering his vision carried further, and applied more clearly. That is what I am trying too: though most of my books are still to write.

Have you tackled Branford's "<u>Science and Sanctity</u>" yet? Pray do!

Indeed may I ask you to put down your impression – in a brief review? The book needs your help badly, and it would be of the greatest encouragement to him, and help too – for the ordinary British and American reviewers can of course make nothing of it – having neither its idealism nor its reconstructive vision and aim, whereas here is a fresh *presentment* of Idealism towards Reconstruction. So I beg: give an hour's writing! (of course making your criticisms freely too.) Pray reply as to this?

You ask me – how (to) find teachers who can see things related? Not easy of course – yet that is what my life's teaching has been, and is here. And I now and then get some one who does more or less grasp this: *e.g.* you will find that Arthur, and now Adrian too, though essentially trained before I got him as a business man, have some ideas of education as in unity and con-specialisms, and no longer mere dis-unity and dis-specialisms. So too with Boshi Sen etc.

Always yours – faithfully

P. Geddes.

[Visva-Bharati letterhead]

2 January 1924

Dear Professor,

During my long absence the burden of unanswered letters and unperformed duties has accumulated to an alarming dimension obstructing my freedom of rest and work. I wish I had, like yourself, the good luck to be rescued from this by the kindly intervention of some illness allowing me shelter in a nursing home.

We have in mind the place of modification in our temple and tank and are waiting for some funds to carry it out. The planting of trees is going on though the lack of sufficient water is making our task difficult. A great part of the dining room has been changed and I hope a better time will come to us when we shall be able to dispose with it altogether.

I have already read, in spite of numerous distractions, a large portion of Branford's Science and Sanctity with a great deal of sympathy and interest. It is a highly suggestive book, very helpful for me as I am in full agreement with the idealism it represents. In fact I was about to ask you to write a review of it for our Visva-Bharati Journal. I could have undertaken to do it myself were I free from some very pressing engagements one of which is preparing lectures for my Chinese tour. The time for my voyage to China is drawing near and yet I have not been able to begin my writing. I feel that I can no longer put it off, though the financial need of our institution may once again drag me off my desk to the quest of money.

Ever yours

Rabindranath Tagore

My dear Geddes,

Your letter written 2 or 3 months ago has followed me about on my journey to the Far East where I went to join the Poet in China. I have just turned it out of my letter case here in Malacca in British Malaya and I am so sorry that it has been remaining unanswered so long.

I entirely agree with you that we are far too much living from hand to mouth at Santiniketan and in danger of doing things (in our construction) piece-meal rather than by developing our main principles first and then planning accordingly. The truth is we have two kinds of people. There are those who have merely conventional ideas of building up another 'university' somehow. They think of what they have learnt at Calcutta or Benares or Bombay. There are others who are genuinely trying to break away from the old bad 'Government' tradition, but have not got much further. Therefore we live (as I have said) a good deal from hand to mouth. All the same we have got a true life within, we have roots. We are not déraciné.

There is nothing that I would like better than to get your own ideas carried forward further than your Indore Report which I studied very carefully indeed and the Poet studied also: indeed he gave it to me to study, saying how good and original and refreshing it was.

I want to make one point clear. I doubt if the Poet has done his own ideal justice by translating the word Visva Bharati by 'University'. Certainly it is a bad translation. Yet I do not quite know what word to use. I feel that it is likely to be more and more a "Settlement" where people come to live a life and form a kind of laboratory for great thinking,[118] – living out as far as they can what they are thinking. Perhaps at one time this was the 'University' ideal itself. But I feel certain that the 'Ashram' of Ancient India is always in the Poet's mind. That is fundamental with him. It is this that makes it very hard for me personally to be at all suggestive or original. I rather look to him to give the lead, and follow the line he takes.

---

[118] One is reminded of Geddes' sociological laboratory at the Outlook Tower in Edinburgh, where international minds met.

But no one more than he welcomes with open arms original suggestions, which come to him and he has a great admiration for you because he always finds you both original and suggestive. In his letter to me from abroad he sent me what he had written about you, and it was published in the Modern Review and will also be published in the new book of 'Letters from Abroad' which is just coming out. He said you are so 'human' and love of science had only increased your love of nature and your 'human' outlook. I am putting it all very badly – while he put it perfectly.

If therefore you are able to write I do hope you will do so and I can assure you that it will be studied and read with utmost care.

I have written this under great distraction in the midst of acute labour and opium problems.

With my very kindest regards

Yours very sincerely

C.F. Andrews

Dear Tagore

I hope you are now returning safely from your South American and Mexican visits? And also, that (though I have no reply as to your plans for the seminar) you are not forgetting your promised visit to Edinburgh, as President of a first "<u>International Congress on University Progress</u>", which I have been preparing for accordingly, as Organising Secretary.

But meantime the immense "<u>World Conference in Education</u>" an organisation of some years standing has taken possession of Edinburgh. It is on the scale of the British Association – with large international membership. Its field is more that of Primary and Secondary Education than of Higher – but it has two days' meetings on University subjects. They have invited me (and also) to come as delegates of our respective institutions – and they ask us to combine with their meeting – offering to give additional scope and meetings for University questions, such as we may wish to raise.

As you have not been within my reach, and I have not had your address, I have had to take decision to accept their terms – and say that I should plead with you to do <u>also</u>, as soon as I could get in touch with you again.

Edinburgh could hardly stand two Educational Congresses in the one season – whereas this arrangement gives you a far vaster audience, who will carry back your message to them to all countries. And even in the short period, we can at least continue the enquiries as to University Progress in the best sense, which can be followed up for future <u>meeting.</u>

The function is fixed for the <u>last week of July</u> – and I very sincerely hope that this time will be convenient for you? Pray reply by letter or wire (telegraphic address = <u>Geddes, Les Brusses. Montpellier</u>).

I have been hard at work building and guarding this new undertaking – continuing not only my old contacts, these 40 years past nearly, with this University; in many ways throughout the past-seven centuries the leading Mediterranean one, and also linking those of Scotland with France, relations which are yet older – as well as deeply important to us still.

Then too, since I am planning for you, I want very much to persuade you to look in here with what I am trying to realise – a more all satisfactory environment for the student; and not only in conditions of health but beauty, of intelligence in general as well as special studies, and in at once more effective yet more meditative life. In a word to build the house not only of the body but of the mind and spirit.

But I am called away from this in three months from now, to go to Jerusalem, to the opening of my first buildings there, as inauguration of the University by Balfour (and I hope also Bergson) to whom the University Committee desires also to add <u>yourself</u>, and thus to obtain your message on Education as it should be, and may be.

I am indeed specially charged by the University Committee, ([illegible] its President, Dr. Eden,) to plead with you to accept; and from two sessions intimate relations in Jerusalem and planning widely over Palestine, and for the City of Jerusalem as well as the University, I can safely assure you of an audience of the right sort not only of Zionists, and of Government etc. (some of whom are accessible to ideas, and even ideals) but also all sections of the Christian and Moslem communities also, of whom the best are not consumed by the mutual hatreds which are as exaggerated by the press, but open to your (and India's) message of mutual tolerance, and even goodwill.

Their invitation is of course being sent you officially; but this as above indicated, is also no less directly theirs: (of course you will be reimbursed of all travelling and other expenses by the University Commission.)

Pray let me hear from you as soon as may be, alike as to <u>Edinburgh for last week of July, and Jerusalem at the end of March, for first days of April.</u>

Believe me

Always yours

Patrick Geddes

Cordial remembrances to Elmhirst, as also to your son if he is with you –
in which Arthur, (who is assisting me here and working on his thesis for
Doctorate) very warmly writes.

PG

Rai A.C. Bose, Bahadur, M.A.
Controller of Examinations
Calcutta University

To
Prof. Patrick Geddes, M.A.
Outlook Tower
Edinburgh
28.2.25

Sir,

I have the honour, by director of the Hon'ble the Vice-Chancellor and
Syndicate, to inform you that you have been appointed a member of the
Board of Examiners, noted in the margin to examine the thesis, submitted
by Mr. Binodbehari Datta, M.A., B.L., in support of his candidature for
the Degree of Doctor of Philosphy. It is requested that you will be so good
as to examine the thesis, in consultation with the 2 other members of the
Board and to favour the Syndicate with a joint report on the result of your
examination. A copy of the thesis entitled "Town Planning in Ancient
India" submitted by the candidate who is a First Class M.A., of this
University (in Mixed Mathematics – later went to Sanskritic Studies) is
being forwarded herewith …a honorarium of Rs. 100/-

I have the honour to be,

Sir,
Your most obedient servant,
A C Bose
Controller[119]

[119] In the left-hand margin there are these printed details: –
Prof. D.R. Bhandakar,
M.A., Ph.D., 35 Ballygunj Circular Road Calcutta
Prof. Patrick Geddes
Outlook Tower
Edinburgh
Dr. P.K. Acharya,
I.E.S., M.A., Ph. D.,
D.Litt.
University of Allahabad,
Allahabad

My dear Geddes,

Your letter with its enclosures was extremely interesting to me and I have been waiting to bring it before the Poet. I expect that you will have read in the papers that he had a relapse of his heart trouble and was strictly forbidden by the doctors to come to Europe. He greatly regrets that he did not defy them all and go to Europe but on the whole I feel the risk would have been too great and the best thing will be to remain quietly at Santiniketan for another six weeks and then come to Europe.

Will you tell Arthur, if he is with you, that his plan of what we call 'Tata Building' has been a very great success. It *crowns* the slight rise of ground beautiful *(sic)* and is wonderfully breezy and cool. The design is almost perfect and we are all delighted with it. The only fault has been that of the local builders who as is not unusual have done their work in a slovenly manner. But on the whole it is a grand success!

I was not able to bring your plan before our Visva Bharati Council before we closed for the holidays. The Pujas[120] came unexceptionally early this year and we broke up before I could do so.

I liked immensely your printed schedule of nature study and your method of getting away from the black and white page to the living thing. I have just been suggesting revolutionising our geography in the school by taking them out and showing them the mountains, lakes and rivers and villages and soil erosions etc. that are to be seen every day during the rains in our laterite soil.

I am sorry to say your new book, with Thomson, in biology never appeared. I have been waiting for it and I should so much like to have it and review it. Do let me have a copy for that purpose if possible.

---

[120] This is the festival of Durga Puja in Bengal, which N.C. Chaudhuri describes as the 'climax of the year'. Following the lunar calendar, like Easter, it varies. It can be anytime either at the end of September or in sometime October. This is vacation time for all institutions. (N.C. Chaudhuri, *The Autobiography of an Unknown Indian*, 1951, Bombay: Jaico Publishing House, 3rd imp., 1969), p. 63.

I will write again later when I have consulted the Visva Bharati authorities. I have been actively taking up 'Opium' and exposing how the revenue, derived from it, is standing in the way of progress. I will send you a Copy of the Assam Report and I should be most grateful if you could place in any social and economic journal a signed review upon it. Give my love to Arthur.

Yours very sincerely

C.F. Andrews

Santiniketan
7 December 1925

Dear Geddes,

I am waiting for the summer for my next voyage to Europe. But this time it will chiefly be for medical treatment. Doctors here have declared my bodily condition as damaged which deprives me of my freedom of movement. I hope that after a few weeks' rest and doctoring in some European Sanatorium I shall be fit again for the kind of service that you claim from me. It has been decided that the first part of my stay in Europe will be spent in a quiet spot in Switzerland where Romain Rolland has promised to arrange for all that I shall need, and then if doctors advise me I shall do a little travelling. Anyhow, your place I am sure to visit – and as for the President's post which you offer I do not have the heart to refuse although I have a profound dislike for taking any conspicuous place in a public function.

Give my love to Arthur

Ever yours

Rabindranath Tagore

Dear Gurudeva,

My greatest pleasure in coming to Paris has been meeting a Santiniketan friend – Mme Hoogman-Karpelés, and hearing of you and finding the life of Santiniketan again, as it were. In particular she has set me playing the airs I noted of your songs, and the deep pleasure they give me has received the desire to get them written out and urged me to do my duty and have them printed. (Forgive my having let them lie so long: I was swamped with work for my father when I arrived in Europe, and have been pretty run down till lately, but am now in good form and well at work at my thesis, which may I hope be written before long.)

I want to ask you <u>what form the printing should take?</u>

Dinu Babu had suggested sending some to a London magazine. But on comparing the amount I have written out I find it just equals A.K. Coomeraswamy's "Thirty songs from the Punjab and Kashmir". I have just 30 songs – 15 from the King of the Dark Chamber and some 15 others.

(They seemed so few beside the wealth of airs you have composed that I thought I was poor, and behold I am rich!) They seem very well worth while making a book of, with translations, so that words and music should be felt together.

If a book, then in what form? The simplest way would be, like in Coomeraswamy's book, to print the airs, to be hummed or strummed, with your free unmetrical translations? and the Bengali words printed (in Roman print?) beside them. Then Bengalis could sing them, those few at least who read our notation. But they could not be sung by Westerners without a metrical translation, fitted to the music. Could you still do that? (I don't think it need be rhymed: the rhythm is the essential.) It would be splendid if they could be sung, introduced to Western hearers by singers who learnt from you. Or failing you I'd do all I could with my fiddle: the oral tradition is the greatest part of our music, still more of a new music from another land.

I wish this could be. I should like the music lovers of the West to know your Indian music and come to feel it akin, and not "strange" to theirs, just as the lovers of poetry come to love the poetry you translated because they felt the human kinship, even more than the difference of dress, (though that added charm and interest and a loveliness of its own.) Might it not be the same for music?

The question of singing has one further difficulty that most Westerners have so lost the sense of pure melody that to them to sing a song or play a melody without accompaniment would be like appearing on a platform with no clothes on! You know that a melody is enough for me, but that is because I was brought up on Scottish airs, and I realize (to my surprise) that other people don't feel as I do. Folk song collectors are faced with the same difficulty. Whereas you (and to some extent I) may feel that an accompaniment is added, most people here feel that an air without a few chords to "place" it has been robbed of something that belongs to it.

I do not think that a very simple accompaniment need do harm. As for our Highland music, written in modes, the chords should stay within the mode, (and then sound fine,) so I think it might be for your melodies. If the chords were kept within the raga or ragini it seems to me that they should help us to hear, not disguise, the melody, – just as a line of veil, a glimpse of colour, may complete and perfect the movement of a dancer. There is also the rhythm given by the drum for the rapidly moving songs, and their characteristic notes of the drums which the piano is well able to suggest. Moreover so much is lost with the starry nights, the landscape, and the plays in which the songs were sung that something is needed to replace or, as it were, "translate" them. And this brings up the point of the plays.

The unity of the plays gave a richness to the songs one misses when sung apart. Would it be possible to write a brief note of the plays from which the songs were taken principally, giving the outline of the play, and placing the song so that it is understood at the culminating point of a wave of emotion, which you expressed in words, action, colour, and melody at its highest point? It was with the idea of keeping the unity that I asked Dinu Babu to sing the airs (or their principal themes) of one whole play (the King of the Dark Chamber).

Would it not be well then, to give with the outline of the three plays from which the songs mainly come, a word of how they were acted and presented, and, better still, a few sketches, from Nanda Lal Babu, Mme Karpelés and others of the artists? Chitra did quite a beautiful colour drawing of the Beggar maid in Sacrifice, of which he must have a block, for it was reproduced, and if better printed might do him better justice. There must be lots of sketches? I tried a few myself, but I think they are too imperfect! Mme Karpelés can tell me.

To return however to the actual melodies, could not the collection be made as complete as possible? Has the music of the airs recorded on the gramophone been <u>written</u> by M. Benoit or others? If not, it should be done: I could do it if you liked, and it would be quite easy for the set of records to be sent by post. Has M. Benoit written down more airs? Should we not join them?

Later: I have shown this note to Mme Karpelés who offers to help all she can and is most eager that you should at last let a collection be made, an anthology of music you feel to be among your best. (– Have I been able to note those you like best? Did I tell you that I had been able to note Pechu de ke[121], the "lament" as we'd say in the Highlands of the most beautiful of them all. I think you know, most of the rest, and Dinu Babu has seen them all and tells me they are correctly noted. But what gives me deepest pleasure, (after your own encouragement was that which friends in Santiniketan gave me in asking me to play them to them.)

Do let me hear from you, by your own hand or by one of your devoted secretaries. Mme Karpelés tells me you hope to be over in June. I wish it were sooner!

One more question, of detail: is there any musician you would specially like to try to make accompaniments, if you approve, as I feel you may? Meantime I shall look about me. Do you trust for instance, my own

---

[121] *Pichhu deke* means 'calling from behind', the first line of a song by Tagore.

musical sense enough to select a musician you would then judge yourself of the result when you came over and decide. But I feel I have lost too much time as it is, and am eager to begin, so as to have something to show you when you come over.

And do you know of an Indian here capable of putting in drum beats in the proper places where they belong? Playing over the series from the "Dark Chamber" last night I felt how much the quieter melodies, sung alone, gained when they came after some joyous shouting and drumming chorus. Some effect of this in the accompaniment of the latter would help the former.

No more just now.

Love and homage from one of your loving chelas[122] in the west

Arthur

---

[122] Chela: disciple, made so memorable by Kiplings' Kim, who attaches himself to the Buddhist Lama as his chela.

College des Ecossais
Plan des 4 Seigneurs
Montpellier
France
28 January 1926

Dear Tagore,

We are sincerely obliged by your acceptance of our Presidency, and we hope you will have no cause to regret it. But after all, a president naturally wants to know what he is president of! – and <u>that</u> I shall be able to show you when you come to Europe.

I very earnestly hope that you will put in your plans a short visit to me at this place. (It is quite easily reached from P.L.M. line north from Marseilles, by which route I trust you will come. You have only one change at <u>Tarascon</u>, the junction north of Arles, and before reaching Avignon.)

I venture to hope also that you will be interested in this new academic endeavour; for we are here at the beginnings of a system of national foundations, which cannot but have influence in this university, and even suggestiveness to others. Already not only American and Zionist groups are beginning, but three Indians are coming into temporary residence here, till we can get a house bought or built for them, as the Indian College. For this is the only university of the whole Mediterranean which is widely attractive to foreign students; and thus it has always had them from many countries, and now more and more. Besides leading in medical, agricultural and natural science, it has also some life as regards the humanities; and regional studies, with Provençal literature, are excellent. I think too you will be interested in my buildings and gardens, and thus we may have that long-delayed talk over <u>your own plans</u>, for kindred purposes, and even more extensive ones!

Besides the above request, I have two others. Your "Parrot's Training" has delighted people here, and some of them want to publish translation in France, here it is also much needed. Can you facilitate this by lending the blocks of illustrations?

One other point. At a recent discussion here, we were all lamenting that though the various revolutionary parties have plenty of songs, the more truly progressive ones are still mostly without them. We especially bewailed the lack of any song which could express the movement of international sympathy and good-will, of which the League of Nations, with all its limitations, is the expression. Yet it is the only most conspicuous among many minor ones, in which we are all living – indeed you especially. So, as the conversation went on, all with one voice agreed that we must ask that needed song from – <u>Tagore</u>! <u>Will you write it</u>? An admirable musician, a true idealist, who is head of our Conservatoire of Music in Montpellier, and an invaluable influence accordingly, will be able not only to get us a good translation into French, by one of our young poets, but will himself do his utmost to set it to European music, if yours proves difficult for us in the west. And so, if some day such a poem comes to you, as we all hope it will, we hope you will let us have it! And I can safely promise that we shall have it well sung to you on your arrival here; while the English version will also be circulated, and I trust translated in the other tongues as well.

I am sure you will pardon me for thus proposing such a task to our president, already so fully occupied; but we shall not trouble you very often.

Yours ever,

P. Geddes

You will also find here many who know and appreciate some at least of your works; and a good many who understand English quite well enough to appreciate a talk from you also. But I can quite understand that your doctor may not approve of any lecturing till you have had your mountain holiday: so I shall protect you from such invitations, and let you rest quietly in my garden. (I have a Heliotherapy corner here! – quite in competition with the Swiss ones!)[123]

---

[123] All the underlining in this typed letter is done by hand. The postscript is added in Geddes' own hand.

Agartala Palace
16 February 1926

Dear Geddes,

I gladly accept the honour done to me by choosing me as your President, though I am sure that I am hopelessly incompetent for such a post.

"Parrot's Training" has already been translated into the Czeck with illustrations. I have often tried to get the blocks from Thackers but have failed. You have no other alternative but to copy the pictures from the English book.

I shall try to write the song you asked from me but you must know that your language does not surrender itself to my muse as easily as my own mother tongue. The initial barrier of diffidence frightens me off from the task.

I hope to be able to secure accommodation in an Italian steamer sailing for Europe on the 15th April next. My first two or three weeks will have to be given to Italy and then from Switzerland I shall come to your place when I have permission from the doctor. My state of health needs immediate attention which I can only have in Europe.

Ever yours

Rabindranath Tagore[124]

---

[124] This letter is written on Rabindranath Tagore's letterhead.

Dear Arthur,

How delighted to have your letter. Do whatever you like with my songs; only do not ask me to do the impossible. To translate Bengali poems into English verse form reproducing the original rhythm so that the words may fit in with the theme would be foolish for one to attempt. All that I can venture to do is render them in simple prose making it possible for a worthier person than myself to versify them. Please write the accompaniment yourself. I can trust you, for you are modest and are not likely to smother my tunes with a ruthless display of your own musical talent. I shall be able to give the outline of the play from which the songs are taken in order to give them their proper background. As for other details, I shall have them discussed when we meet in Europe.

Just now I am busy touring in East Bengal. It is perfectly unwise from medical point of view but their are other points of view in its favour which it has been difficult for me to ignore.

But I am tired and am longing to give up missions of all kinds and merely to share the life and impulse of the trees and birds in this delightful springtime redolent of mango blossoms.

With love,

Yours affectionately,

Rabindranath Tagore

Greeting to Morris and old friends

Dear Gurudev,

It gave me such pleasure to hear from you, and to know you liked the idea of a book of songs. Now for the realisation – perhaps when you come over to Europe?

I hope you may be well, well enough, at least, to rest and travel quietly by summer time? I have just seen that you are ill, but I do so earnestly hope for a quick recovery.

I am just over in London to bring a bit of my thesis up to the point, and get it criticised. There are one or two men here really interested in India and its people, and I've learnt quite a lot from them, a little of which I hope to return.

Have I told you that I'm trying to learn and tell something about Bengal Rural Life and Villages? You, with a life-time spent among your people, may well smile! Let me say (in part defence) that it was people over here who urged me to do it. Those who know most have said least, and it is left to people like me to unravel and tell something about the soil and civilisation of your land. How I wish I could talk to you of these things, and hear of your long love and knowledge of Bengal. I have (unexpectedly) learnt many things about Bengal, and where I think I understand better, I should like to know your thought, so much.

With affectionate greeting and wishes of recovery

from your loving

Arthur

Dear Gurudev,

I have seen a friend, Mme C.M.A. Peake, who has done translations of Japanese poetry, which are themselves delightful as poetry, and I believe are faithful to the spirit of the original, for she lived in Japan and did them with Japanese friends. I told her of our scheme of publishing your songs and she said, "Oh, could I help to put them into verse? Would the Poet come and stay here while we worked at them? I have long loved his poems, and would love to do this!" She is now bringing out a book of her own verse, but when that is done, in 2 months or so, Peake would be free, and I know of no one so good. I must ask her to send you a copy of her Japanese translations: I feel sure you will like them, "Sword and Blossom Songs", they are called, – 3 little volumes, brought out by a Japanese publisher.

(2) I have just seen the music publisher for Humphrey Guilford, (Oxford University Press) who is interested and may take it up. He is a friend of the Peakes, who sent me to him.

He likes the whole thing, and the idea of possible illustrations – (by Nanda Lal Bose, Miss Karpelés and others?) of which I spoke in my last letter.

I shall write again telling of progress, and meantime send my love and good wishes for rest and the life you would like to lead,

Very affectionately from

Arthur[125]

---

[125] There is a note on the top left-hand corner of this letter which reads, 'Requested to wait until Gurudeva's visit to Europe – M.' One can only surmise that the 'M.' might stand for 'Mahalanobis', and in that case, one may wonder if the 'request' is on medical grounds or not, given Tagore's fragile state of health at this time.

[Montpellier seal]

College Des Ecossais
Plan Des Quatre Seigneurs
Montpellier[126]
5 May 1926

Dear Tagore,

I am called to send on enclosed – and I can say I believe it to be a desirable venture: at present however I am telling them that I do not think your physician would allow you to take such trouble. So <u>unless you have someone to recommend</u> you need not trouble replying at present.

I was sorry to see in the papers, soon after receiving your letter announcing intended visit to Europe this season, that you were not so well. I hope however that you are better again and that the proposed visit may come off all right, and with good result.

My Indian students here are doing well Advani and Shivdasani have each got their "<u>D.Litt</u>" for good theses, the first with "<u>Mention Honorable</u>", for a Study of Sind (and comparison with S. France) and the second with "<u>Mention Très Honorable</u>" for his thesis on <u>Education</u> in India, its needs included. (These "mentions" = 2nd and 1st class Honours respectively, and not often given.) The two others – one a Parsi B.A. from Oxford, P. Bharucha, and my son Arthur – are coming on shortly. also *(sic)* the fifth resident, from my Outlook Tower in Edinburgh is nearly ready also – so <u>all</u> will have done well: a good beginning, while another Indian will be ready next year with his thesis.

I mention the above also because they are preparing to inform the Indian public of their start as a "<u>College des Indians</u>" here, and to invite students etc. This gives a far better introduction to Europe than to land at once in London Oxford or Edinburgh. They can go then afterwards – and with better reception there, when also graduates here, (as they can be with a single year's good work after their Indian studies). The French language has

---

[126] Letterhead.

also a great value, at once for clearing the mind, for access to its great literature, and its wealth of ideas – more than at present in any University Centre in Britain (I hope some day you will speak to people here: we can get you an audience to understand you in English.) So send us a good student!

With all good wishes

Always yours

P. Geddes

P.S. I am hopeful of considerable developments here – and in which your ideas and ideals have an effective share. Even practical application; as for waking up the greatest of Mediterranean Schools of Agriculture by the example of Surul's influence in surrounding villages. I have bought a fine old chateau – both medieval and renaissance – for extensions here, and with this am preparing a large example of afforestation, (as I hope you are not forgetting for stopping the spread of the desert around you!)

What of the University plans? I am going north next month, and planning for Bristol University – and perhaps also for the nascent scheme for the Scottish Highlands. Your promised Song will encourage them all there as here, and elsewhere. We are also building actively at Jerusalem, for my partner and son-in-law, Mears.

PG

Sun 29 May 1926

Dear Tagore,

I am very glad to hear from Elmhirst that he is meeting you at Naples. I wrote you to Santineketan last week! So may I venture to repeat the hope that you (and he too) may be able to pay us even a short visit here on your way northward to Switzerland? Here (as also at a neighbouring medieval and renaissance chateau and indeed at other points) there are beginnings of University undertakings carrying forward previous plannings whether at Edinburgh or Chelsea, or at Jerusalem, and Santiniketan etc; so I am hopeful they may interest you – and the more since, among them, we are at the beginning of our Indian College. For the Mediterranean region, and even this one of its various universities in particular, affords a better start point for Indian students coming to Europe than can those of the North; and moreover after a year or so here, and the Doctor's degree which our Indian graduates here are already taking, they will get far more attention from their teachers in British Universities than do the embarrassing members of junior Indians as undergraduates at present.

So for this Indian College here we hope for your benediction when you come – and even as an *element* in the League of Academic Nations which every great University should develop for and with its students from all countries more or less, as so much here.

With all good wishes and hopes alike for your own recovery of health and strength and for your world widening influence,

Yours ever

P. Geddes

[Montpellier seal]

COLLEGE DES ECOSSAIS
PLAN DES QUATRE SEIGNEURS
MONTPELLIER[127]

29 May 1926

Dear Elmhirst,

Very glad to have your letter, and to learn that all goes well with you. Congratulations very particularly to Mrs. Elmhirst, and yourself – and on the good fortune of a daughter! (It is one of my regrets to have only one, and that she has only boys!)

I am enclosing this in a letter to the Poet (which I hope may reach him!) Pray realise that this place is very easily reached. Through carriage from Marseilles in the Toulouse-Bordeaux section of most P.L.M. trains northward. And when the train is obviously for Paris the change is at Tarascon (first stop after Arles and before Avignon) where a train is always waiting and with short run. You and the Poet too will be interested in the place on its little hilltop of varied terrace gardens and wild heath with extensive outlook between Sea and Cevennes (and even Pyrenees and Alps when mornings clearest): also in our new acquisition of medieval and late Renaissance chateau a bit inland from here, as [illegible] possibilities of University developments from caverns to city-centres. And I hope too for his and your interest in the nascent Indian College of which first circular is enclosed to the Poet with this.

Yours ever

P Geddes[128]

---

[127] On Montpellier letterhead.
[128] In a postscript in the left-hand margin, Geddes adds, '(Wire if I may meet you at Station here.)'

Le Grand Hotel et de Rome[129]
31 May 1926

25.6.26[130]

My dear Arthur,

We landed yesterday in Naples and I hasten to drop you these few lines to let you know that we are here and shall be glad to hear from you or your father advising us as to the most suitable time to visit the Montpellier University. Our programme has not been fully made up yet – so father will be free to accept any time that is convenient to Dr. Geddes. We remain a week here and visit Florence and Turin on our way to Switzerland. We are arranging to spend a few days with Romain Rolland at Villeneuve and then we are free.

Could you kindly ask your father whether he knows of some sort of international gathering at Cambridge this summer? Father has been asked to speak there but he should like to know some detail informations regarding this conference.

Elmhirst came down to meet us – and we are so glad to meet him again.

With best greetings to your father and yourself, I remain

Yours sincerely

Rathindranath Tagore

---

[129] The address is part of the hotel letterhead.
[130] This date is noted at the top left-hand corner of the letter.

[Montpellier letterhead]

Tuesday morning 1926[131]

Dear Tagore,

Your telegram just received, and I reply – as, "detained Scotland till end September, University closed till end October. Try end June or first week July." Geddes

I'll postpone departure from here, if necessary, till after first week of July: so pray try come. Very sorry to crowd your arrangements, but we shall let you rest here, and reduce University contacts to an afternoon garden party or so, if you do not feel equal to a big meeting at the University. But your presence and impulse will be felt and appreciated by all.

Let me know how your plans proceed. This place is quite easily reached: from Marseilles, there are usually through carriages, marked *Cette Toulouse-Bordeaux*, but by trains [illegible] you have to change at Tarascon, from which a short run here.[132]

---

[131] This is written by Geddes, probably in the latter half of June. Tagore was in Italy from the end of May (as Rathindranath's letter of 26 May 1926 to Arthur, from Naples, implies). Tagore himself is still optimistic about coming to Montpellier in his letter of 27 June 1926 (which he writes from Villeneuve, where he had settled after leaving Italy on 22 June 1926), though his plans are still open. (See Dutta and Robinson, 1995), p. 269.
[132] This is probably a rough draft, heavily crossed out towards the end, unfinished and unsigned.

Dear Tagore,

Sorry you can't manage before 26th. but as my last letter indicated, I can wait another fortnight or so for you. So can't you still manage that? A mere talk between us in London or elsewhere is no substitute. For here are definite beginnings, of interest for you – and even with bearings on Santineketan and its planning – developments in various ways ahead of all my previous schemes in India and Europe, or in Palestine either.

For instance, the collegiate development on international scale – towards (League) Society of Academic Nations – yet so becoming freed of "nationalism" in its bad senses. This largely too by our incipient Indian College, and this as better start point for our Indian graduates than they find in London or Edinburgh – in Oxford or Cambridge. Better because here is what has long been one of the most international of universities. Better also because in peculiarly complete environment – of representative (and monumentally impressive) survivals – as from early cavern life to pre-Roman and Roman, through Frankish and Medieval times, and through Renaissance in its various developments to XVIII century, and thence again to the French Revolution and its consequences all far more fully and intelligibly than elsewhere and within moderate area in Europe, (even Italy not excepted), so that you will find your own understanding of Western history and culture intensified and clarified, let alone the Indian student's. For in our great cities he finds himself submerged from the first, with their immense modern industrial imperial or financial developments, not only obscuring for him the better elements of our cultural past, but concealing, in most cases almost completely, our incipient renewals and elements of progress which he commonly fails to get into touch with.

Here amid this most intelligible of introductions to Western Civilisation – for which this University region is the best I have found – and in lifelong wanderings through those of most other countries also – Indian students are better prepared for Britain etc. For after their year or so of intensive work, (and in the most brain-clearing of western languages) and with their doctor's degree, they will also find far more help and attention from our best teachers than these have time and encouragement to give among numerous juniors.

You will see thus how we have been looking forward to your visit, and with hopes that you would thus feel justified in approving our further development as of definite value to Indian students in Europe.

Returning to Santiniketan planning – and in relation to that for various other Universities also – you will we hope be interested in various endeavours here towards presentments of the sciences *i.e.* in more definite co-operation than elsewhere with the "humanities", and with socialised applications too – from city to village renewal – as and from horticulture and agriculture to the afforestation I so eagerly pled with you for – In all this too your suggestions and encouragements would alike be of greatest value.

Then too your influence is needed in France, and at another centre besides Paris; while from this your impulse would peculiarly reach throughout the other (16!) provincial universities – for which we should have your talk in English reported, translated and diffused. Here your visit is already eagerly looked forward to by many worth your helping: pray do not disappoint them! Pardon then my importunateness.[133]

---

133 The end of this letter is missing.

College des Ecossais
Plan des 4 Seigneurs
Montpellier France
26 June 1926

Dear Rathi,

Many thanks for writing to me. Your letter was given me when I arrived, and had been already answered. Still I want to say how much I too hope that you and your father will be able to come here. The term begins again about 1st Nov. but I understand that many people come back even in October, though not all, and you would even find people to welcome you, and of course we should be here.

I am also very keen to put the Bengali words and prose translations of your father's melodies together. It would also be worth while writing out some of those from the 'King of the Dark Chamber' of which I have only a summary. And finally it would be worth while my writing down some of the slower airs which I have not yet written down, for looking over the 30 airs I have noted I find that perhaps an undue portion are the light, merry tunes which I noted because they were simple and everybody sang them. To do justice to Gurudeva, there should be a few more of the slower, and deeper airs like "Bairobi", and "Pichu Daké –". This is why I asked if you would have the photograph records if taken, with you here. Have you got them? If not, can you write for them?

All this will take time, and demands (what I should so much like to do), a meeting to work over these together.

And with this goes Mrs. Peake's invitation to your father to stay and try over the translations and make verses for the tune. Morris has just returned her book of poems which I'd sent to Santiniketan, which will show you what she has done. I'm keeping it till I hear from you where it can find you!

And while we are together I should like very much indeed to submit my notions of a study of the soil and civilisation of Bengal to yourself, and to your father. This is what I've been working at for the last year, and it's taken me far further than I expected. I've now got a good deal written and ready for initial criticism and review, and there is no one whose help would be so valuable as your father's and your own.

When then can we meet and talk of these projects – and carry them out? If your father cannot come over here yet, can you? And where is Pratima Devi? And that black-eyed, naughty darling, Poupée?

My only fixture is to go to Domme (Dordogne, France) Aug 21st – Sept 5th or Sept 21st – Oct 5th. I intend to stay in France till November, chiefly because it's cheaper, and I must return here in Nov. to pass my doctorate.

As to publishing, Macmillan's are "considering" the idea of your father's melodies, (and likewise of my own, Bengal study). The Oxford University Press had the airs for some time but turned them down; in doing so, however, they made the useful suggestion that the airs should be launched by a singer (? Miss McCarthy perhaps?)

With warmest greeting to your father, Pratima Devi and other friends,

Your friend ever

Arthur

PS My father asks me to enclose these particulars of the Cambridge studies, in answer to his enquiry for your father. I understand that both the university and the city (*i.e.* the Mayor, and the university men), would have be glad to welcome your father, and will be when he can come, though it needn't be on any imposing scale or in a fatiguing way.

Hotel Byron,
Villeneuve.
27 June 1926.

Dear Geddes,

Your letter has just reached me after a long delay, redirected from Rome. I want to meet you and have a talk with you about the institution with which you are connected. I am sure it will be easy for me to persuade our young students who want to pursue their studies in Europe to join this University. Please let me know in details about the expenses of living and tuition and also the subjects of study. If you have any printed literature it will be of use. Cannot Arthur write a detailed description of the Institution for the Modern Review, discussing the advantages which an Indian student may enjoy in this place? I shall try to induce some of our own students to come there and if you have one he will attract others. This will give an international atmosphere.

Ever yours

Rabindranath Tagore.

Scottish Women's Club Ltd.
95A George Street
Edinburgh[134]

38 Rue Ringham Terrace
28 June 1926

Dear Professor Geddes,

I see in the Sunday Observer an interview with Rabin. *(sic)* Tagore in which it is mentioned that he is to lecture in Italy, Paris and London. Nothing is said of Edinburgh but last summer we hoped he might be here and that we could arrange a lecture on behalf of the Tower. I am anxious to get the debts paid off during my period of chairmanship and the way made clear and simple for running the Tower, without loss. If this can't be done we must give it up. We were glad to receive a bundle of notices about the Scots College and hope something may come of those you sent to Miss Molyneaux.

Yours in haste

Jean C. Cunningham

---

[134] Letterhead

Dear Rathi,

Since writing the enclosed to your father, your own letter has come, telling me you are leaving for Zurich and Vienna. If you still think we may meet I may add that I expect to be free for sometime. My Bengal thesis etc. will take sometime still and I must return for my "exam" in October-November. I shall probably stay in France and after leaving Domme (Dordogne) that is, after September 5th. or so. I may have a short time with Prof. Sion of this university, my professor and friend, probably in the Pyrenees, and return to Montpellier about October 1st.

I hope you will find your tour interesting and fruitful.

Best wishes to Prasanta: I do not expect to be in Paris for some time or I should like so much to have seen your wife. Oh and thank you for saying you'll look at my Bengal stuff. I really want you to, if you can.

Ever yours

Arthur

I hope your father won't find it tiring to sing over his songs to me, when we do meet. I think I can write them faster than I used to. But have you got the gramophone record?

Dear Geddes,

I do not know if you have already heard from some newspaper report that some time ago I fell ill in Vienna and doctors strongly advise me to take a long detour in order to reach Marseilles from this part of Europe as I am compelled to avoid Italy where they are ready to insult me owing to my letter against Fascism that appeared in the Manchester Guardian. This is a mischance that I never anticipated and I had booked my passage from Marseilles which I had to cancel at the last moment. I cannot tell you how sorry I feel to disappoint you and miss the opportunity of having a talk with you before I leave Europe. I am thoroughly exhausted physically and materially and must hasten back to India to recoup myself. Europe is too expensive for me, the amount of life and means that she claims from one is not in my power to give though she is an inspiration to me in various ways for which I am thankful. I have had a most generous welcome from her which has been a cause of constant surprise to me. I hope it is not a case of overpayment for which a readjustment of accounts will have to be made in future. I do not know when we shall meet again and where. In the meanwhile allow me to assure you of a very warm regards for yourself

Ever yours

Rabindranath Tagore

Give my love to Arthur

[Montpellier seal]

COLLEGE DES ECOSSAIS
PLAN DES QUATRE SEIGNEUR
MONTPELLIER[135]

12 March 1927

Dear Tagore,

We were of course greatly disappointed – as indeed was City and University also – that you could not come: but the news of your better health and renewed dramatic activity makes us hope you may possibly come to us next year?

You will be pleased to hear that Arthur has at length presented his thesis – "Au Pays de Tagore" – and has got his Doctorat-es-Letters (D. Litt.) *(sic)* with highest honours, and regrets from the Jury of examiners that more could not be added! This is a careful and restrained geographical study, as its sub-title implies – The rural civilisation of Western Bengal and its geographical factors. It has been closely looked after by the Professor of Geography (Sion) who is the best French student of India, and also by the botanist, Prof. Flahault, who is our leading French re-afforester. Then too he has connected this with the teaching of Dr. Bentley: as to the connection of malaria with all other geographical and social deterioration. This very much bears out both our pleadings with you, to set agoing as far as may be (1) the re-afforestation of the Khoai land, and (2) of the better land adjacent to it, so as to resist the same fatal attacks, which so shocked me, you remember, on my study of your area, *e.g.* with Cheape's Bungalow area as but an example of what threatens you everywhere. I submit for your consideration the useful application of Western science – in its synthetic and not merely analytic form – to Eastern problems. So, as you have been good enough to promise to send us some good students, this indicates some of the ways in which they might study here, with use to India. Arthur is no doubt sending you a copy, as soon as inclusion of a preface by one of the French geographers allows: and he is also thinking of an English version extended more fully. The difficulty is to find a publisher – since neither in India nor in Britain is there such a market for what seems but

---

[135] This is part of the Scots College letterhead.

"dry" scientific treatment – though fundamentally directed to human issues; but I daresay if he can prevail on you to write a brief preface, indicating your recognition of that, it may induce a publisher to face the risk?

Now another, and yet larger question – that of University Planning, (on which we have always failed to have that serious talk the subject needs – and each of us also.) For a material plan is but the outcome of the life, thought and purpose underlying it – and thus too commonly – as Universities go – of the deficiency of these! So all my life I have been at the thesis symbolised by my three doves (   )[136], in vital order as Sympathy, Synergy and Synthesis – Heart, Hand and Head – Good, Beautiful and True – though in academic order Synthesis takes the highest place. I don't know how far this long quest of western science – from Pythagoras to Plato – Aristotle to Aquinas – from Bacon and Descartes to Leibnitz and the Encyclopedists, and thence to Comte and Spencer etc, has appealed to you: but for University purposes and improvement, it is surely one of the essentials: and so a main problem of all my thinking since early student days; and I trust with some advances accordingly. First that the fields of science in clearer, fuller and more intimate theoretic harmony – of concrete and abstract, of cosmic and human, of naturalistic and social. Hence orderly studies (a) from mathematics, astronomy and geography, physics and biology, to the social sciences; yet likewise (b) back again – *i.e.*, from social origins and activities as a main source of scientific progress from earliest to modern and opening times. Thus with practical as intellectually significant accordingly – the pragmatic doctrine summed up as <u>Vivendo discimus</u> – we learn by living. Thus "<u>Studia Synthetica</u>", in harmony and interaction with "<u>Agenda Synergica</u>", – and more fully than as yet are the "Arts" studies with the old professional "Faculties".

Yet here is where the religious and the philosophical spirits, as well as the poetic and artistic, are so often repelled by our scientific presentment; which seems to them but materialistic – even at its most unified presentment, of social and organic life in nature, and all in mathematical

---

[136] There are three doves sketched here (   ), which together form the famous Geddesian symbol standing for the three s's, signifying Sympathy, Synergy and Synthesis (as he says in this letter).

measure and number so far as may be. For these ask us – what have you to say of ethics, psychology, esthetics, and even logic? – are you not leaving out the good, true and beautiful, for which we essentially care, and so offering us a presentment which remains but mechanical?

That, we must confess, has too much been true of science – and still too often. But here sympathise with its difficulties – its liability to error! It can but proceed from observation to interpretation, and therefore, as far as may be, from simple to complex, and from concrete to abstract, from objective to subjective. Hence then Comte's and others working order of the sciences, the physical before the biological, and these before the social, as most difficult and complex.

Yet the attraction of the physical world – as alike from heavens to landscape – has from the first days of science been by its beauty, its esthetic appeal: while conversely, song and music came clearly into physical science with Pythagoras, and light and colour with Newton. The observation of animal life by earliest hunting-peoples, with which zoology began, was psychological as well was artistic; while social life is by its very nature ethical. Mathematics too is but logic, becoming quantitative. Hence, the graphic presentment of the sciences in Arthur Thomson's and my little "Biology" (pages 144-5) (and now laid out in enduring pavement upon this college terrace), unifies all that is legitimate in materialism and vital in idealism. We thus avoid the divergent extremes of their past presentment, each missing real life – witness a "biology" too much confined to the dissection of the corpse, and a "psychology" in pursuit of a disembodied "mind", thus mere ghost – sans eyes, sans voice, sans everything!

Here I think, we are fundamentally at one in principle, despite all differences in expression? Notably in the idea of converging our studies, our surveys of the fields of knowledge, upon the service of the community life – at present so depressed – in east and west alike – and so towards Vita Sympathetica, and this beyond our existing beginnings of academic residence etc, and in touch with our Villages.

Here our college is already modifying place, work, and so far reaching people, in this suburban Village, just outside the city: while our Chateau further out, has been for a thousand years the centre of its typical rural village – and is now beginning to change from heavy burden on it to helpful group: one increasingly worthy, we hope, of visitors from Santiniketan and Surul, and if possible here and there suggestive to them in turn. For this reaches out, in small beginnings, but large principles, towards the valorisation of rural France, as yours to the corresponding renewal of Bengal. And indeed, if we can help in Bengal and in France, are we not in principle, dealing with Asia and Europe – and finding their needs and possibilities more and more at one? Broadly speaking, the old village problem is much the same in East and West: and, differently though their various historic governments have mismanaged them, their renewal has very much the same tasks.

But if so, we are substantially at one in social action and this always growing more clearly and fully. So too essentially in our thought, our studies of man and nature, and thus our endeavours of organising knowledge more adequately for education purposes, in university and school.

With such substantial unity and harmony, alike in thought and action, mutual sympathy cannot but develop – and further strengthen these. Thus Vita Sympathetica – and not only in each of our academic groupings, but between them, and so across the world, and back again: always more and more of cultural intercourse, and impulse of cooperative activities, of good understanding and good-will, extending from individual friendships and social harmonies, and to racial sympathies.

Finally now a word of practical cooperation. Recall that Conference on University Progress which was to have been held at Edinburgh in 1925 (and under your Presidency) had you been able to attend: but which amalgamated with the International Congress of Education there, about same time. M. Otlet, of the International Bibliographic Institute etc. at Brussels – one of the ablest educational pioneers in Europe – was deputed, along with me, to prepare reports for the next Congress in 1927 (at Toronto),

(1) on better organisation of Universities.

(2) "   " order of studies, both naturalistic and humanistic.

(3) "   " simplification of nomenclature, bibliography etc.

You will see that these are large undertakings! Only brief abstracts for next year, but we trust fuller for the subsequent Congress later. Meantime our organisation already includes (1) Otlet's immense activities (and buildings) at Brussels, mine (2) at Edinburgh, and (3) here, and (4) Branford's at London (LePlay House, Sociological Society, Tours etc.) and (5) the School of Archaeology and Regional Survey established with help of Prof. Reclus and M. Peyrony in the leading European centre of such studies, in Dordogne. Thus we are a nucleus of cooperation, and we seek similar contacts with kindred groups. You must have had experience of these: so it would be a help if you would let your secretary jot down for us such names and addresses as you think of, and authorise me to write to them with our programme as it develops, and with such practical introduction from you? In this way your Presidency of Progressive Educationalists and "idealo-praxists" would be increasingly valuable to us all; and your leadership strengthened, with better understanding of Santiniketan also, here in the West.

With best wishes for your recuperation, and your return – perhaps next year, – Believe me always, respectfully and affectionately yours

P. Geddes

P. S. Arthur before leaving desired me to send his respects and love. He is hopefully awaiting your promised translations of the songs for which he has your music. This will be another of your valued contributions to our European world: for translations into other languages will also soon be wanted. A fine thing to set all the world singing!

UNIVERSITÉ
DE MONTEPELLIER

MONTPELLIER, le 13 Juin 1928

Monsieur,

En réponse à la lettre que vous avez bien voulu m'écrire, j'ai l'honneur de vous informer que je me suis entretenu avec M. le Doyen Vianey et avec M. le Professeur Sion, des dispositions à prendre en vue de la visite que vous m'annoncez. Vous savez les difficultés matérielles que rencontre, à ce moment de l'année, l'organisation de toute conférence, mais l'intérêt que M. Rabindranath Tagore veut bien porter à notre Université nous est trop précieux pour que nous ne fassions pas tout le possible en vue de répondre a son désir. M.M. Vianey et Sion ont bien voulu se charger de prévoir les arrangements nécessaires, que je suis heureux d'approuver.

Veuillez agréer, Monsieur, l'assurance de ma considération très distinguée.

Le Recteur[137]

Monsieur le Professor Geddes.

---

[137] The signature is illegible.

Dear Prof. Geddes,

Gurudev, Rabindranath Tagore, has asked me to write to thank you for your letter of the 7th July. I must apologise for leaving it unanswered so long. He has been keeping very poor health and is in Calcutta now for medical treatment. Nothing serious is the matter with him but he is rather exhausted and Sir Nilratan has prescribed complete rest for him. That is why I am writing to you. His plans for the coming year are still uncertain. He is slowly regaining his strength but unless he is fully restored he may find the journey to Europe somewhat trying. And in any case he may not be able to go about very much. But he would certainly be glad to address the students at the Indian College if he goes to Europe next year. We shall know definitely what his plans are, early next year or towards the end of this year. In any case nothing can be settled till Rathindranath returns from England. I hope you will hear from the Poet himself towards the end of this year what his plans are.

Yours truly

A.K. Chandra

President
Dr. Rabindranath Tagore
Vice Presidents
Sir Jagadish Chandra Bose
Sir Michael Sadler
Sir Brajendranath Seal
Chairman of Executive
The Mayor of Montpellier
Directors
Prof. Patrick Geddes
Mr. E.B. Havell
Secretary
Dr. G.G. Advani

INDIAN COLLEGE
PLAN DES QUATRE SEIGNEURS
MONTPELLIER
22 August 1929

Dear Tagore,

Last night I was reading again your "Creative Unity", and with fresh interest and renewed pleasure. How I wish I could put ideas as you do! We have ideas, that need also to be expressed, but (for lack of the Love-Unity, I fear) expression is lacking!

But now also a business reason for writing – indeed more than one! First Dr. Advani (illegible)[138] brought back enough money (1/2 lakh) from Bombay to start building of Indian College on a fine site on rising edge of garden into health, and with wide views in all direction, from snows to sea, over wilderness, into forest, over city. So now the foundation stone has to be laid, some day after the beginning of October. Alas, that you can't do it! We have therefore called Sir Chimanlal Setalvad, late Vice-Chancellor of Bombay University and very helpful in this matter) who is in London this summer, to do this as he goes southward on way home to India, early in October.

---

[138] Could be abbreviation of 'our secretary'

So will you (our President!) send us a word of benediction, – a verse – a students' song – or what you will – whatever may come to you? I need not say how it will be valued!

Furthermore, can you send us a <u>student</u>? It is most important to make a good start with the spirit and atmosphere of the place; and a young man who has those at Santiniketan is the right one for this! Pray do think of this! I venture to hope he will come back to you all the better for the change. The effectiveness of the German University in the last century (and especially before 1870-1) was deeply aided by the students' <u>migrations</u> from University to University, City to City, teacher to teacher too… like the medieval craftsmen at best. Dr. Stresemann is, by common consent of other nations, the most satisfactory of German Statesmen to deal with, (and so the best for his own country too); and this largely because, as a student, he spent a happy time in Geneva, the second city of French Culture – and so came to appreciate it, instead of hating it, as Prussians too commonly have done.) So our little "<u>Cité Universitare</u>", of increasingly varied type national <u>names</u>, – with free and full intermixture with each other, and with the best we can find of French students too – is an example of what is needed, and increasingly possible, in many Universities; so producing not only Europeans, out of our Nationalists, but bringing together East and West as well, and at their best, essentially as you are showing at Santiniketan.

You may ask how we put students up, with only a foundation laid? We have added this past your twenty or more rooms to the Scots College: so we have now rooms for 33 students in all, and a good big dining-hall, library etc. so there will be no difficulty. Our garden of 6 acres has now 7 more of heath beside, and with no bounds to separate us from the heaths and forest beyond: while at the Chateau du Assas, a few miles out, there is similar accommodation within, and even more space without: a place for holidays – and for history too.

Then too, I'll be 75 by opening of term – and though still in good health and working power, that can't last! Send me someone <u>soon</u>!

You wish contact with Western science; and we have it here, at this University as well among ourselves. More living science, history too, and geography as well, and one of the best traditions and atmospheres in medicine, and even in law! etc. – But the _essential claim_ is that we are all here far less dominated by _urban thought and mechanistic science_, and far more by rural thought and biologic science, and this in its humanised and social forms – and increasingly in applications: – as already in two villages, this one and Assas – and with ambitions probing to the one between: for then we shall have s suggestive centre for more. So again you see your example of Surul is having its effect beyond its immediate range.

I don't often bother you with my attempts at writing: but I venture to send you my last two papers to Sociological Society, and in its Review – which I hope you may have time to glance through. (The reference to Election was only to meet Editor's wish to catch readers!) In this number too, I venture to call your attention to my reviews of _Freud_ (pyscho-analysing the psycho-analyst), of _Zimmerand's_ Wealth versus Thought, and [illegible]ier on Current Progress. (The New Man) and Playne on The Pre-War Mind: – all, I think, in essential sympathy with your views – points and presentments. Our general endeavours, in this little London and Edinburgh group of social students, (Branford and others) is of course to get beyond the _mechanistic_, _pecuniary_, and this Militant pseudo-civilisation of the Industrial Age, and towards that of Life-teaching; (Biotechnics), of world-mending (Geotechnics, _e.g._ Willcock's Irrigation-antidote to the badly mis-engineered malaria of Bengal) and with renewed village and town life (as Etho-Polity –) such as you are initiating around you. In short term, surely some further harmony of East and West? – And alike in thought and action – dream towards deed.

Always yours

P. Geddes[139]

---

[139] This letter is written on the Montpellier letterhead.

President
Dr. Rabindranath Tagore
Vice Presidents
Sir Jagadish Chandra Bose
Sir Michael Sadler
Sir Brajendranath Seal
Chairman of Executive
The Mayor of Montpellier
Directors
Prof. Patrick Geddes
Mr. E.B. Havell
Secretary
Dr. G.G. Advani

INDIAN COLLEGE
PLAN DES QUATRE SEIGNEURS
MONTPELLIER[140]

Montpellier
21 October 1929

Dear Tagore,

Sincere thanks and from each and all – Indians of course first, but all of us too – for your kindness in sending us the poem for our foundation-stone day. Nothing better could we have desired than such stimulus to thought below the surface of things where it is so easy to remain – and here in the West especially!

Yet with gratitude also for favours to come! It would be a great joy to have a song from you some day, not for us particularly, but for the Indian Student in Europe – at once to remember his homeland, yet also to remember to look for and bring back to it from the West, not its defects and limitations sometimes, but such qualities as you once and again generously recognised, and Jagadish Bose too, in his own way, and others.

---

[140] 'College Des Ecossais' and all other details crossed out on this except for the part pertaining to the Indian College letterhead.

148

I quite realise that Santiniketan can't afford to give scholarships here, but if we raise money enough to have one, I can imagine no better use than to ask your help to choose a right occupant among your students. I hope a visit from <u>Boshi Sen</u>[141] on his return from U.S.A. Fine fellow! His science is not merely physico-chemical and physiological though first rate at that: it is vitalised, moralised and socialised, even religionised more than in any other student or young researcher I have known before in any country. (Might he not become a help to you in Santiniketan?)

Our foundation-stone fete has had to be put off – as Sir Chimanlal Setalvad was recalled urgently to India! We are going on building – and if you come to Europe again next spring, I hope you may be able to give us that long hoped visit.

With renewed thanks, and all good wishes

Yours ever

P. Geddes

---

141 The sketch of Geddes by an Indian artist, which we have on the front cover of this book, was given by Boshi Sen to Geddes' granddaughter, Claire Geddes, when she visited him in India, quite by chance.

President
Dr. Rabindranath Tagore
Vice Presidents
Sir Jagadish Chandra Bose
Sir Michael Sadler
Sir Brajendranath Seal
Chairman of Executive
The Mayor of Montpellier
Directors
Prof. Patrick Geddes
Mr. E.B. Havell
Secretary
Dr. G.G. Advani

INDIAN COLLEGE
PLAN DES QUATRE SEIGNEURS
MONTPELLIER[142]

Montpellier, le 20 November 1929

Dear Poet and Honoured Friend,

(Yours of Oct. 31) I quite understand: you will let me know if and when you can come.

Yes, <u>pray</u> write something – in Visva-Bharati or where you think fit – of your ideals and aims in Santiniketan School and University! For that will be at once (1) an impulse to education over the wide world – and (2) a document of testamentary value to your successors, towards continuing and developing your initiatives there, instead of "tying them up in the napkin", as successors often do. That happened not only in Jesus' parable, but in the resultant Christian Church, beginning from St Paul, and continued too much to this day. It is the tragedy of initiatives that the disciples close and enshrine the teaching of their master. That has happened in every religion, has it not? Thus, had not the last Sikh Guru done himself *(sic)*, where might not the Sikhs be now – with still growing scriptures!

---

[142] Indian College letterhead.

150

In science too, despite its "progress", the same thing too often happens; and in philosophy no less. Thus from Descartes came the modern mechanistic obsessions; and from Newton an absolutism which has had to wait for Einstein to relativise it. From Linnaeus (whose "System of Nature" gave the "Principia" of the world of Nature) the evolutionists, from Buffon to Darwin and onwards, have found it hard to escape! And so too for Darwin, since most Darwinians hardened into mechanists and "struggle-for-lifers" (as the French call the idealising wars, and master-castes, and all other devilments of competition. So too Comte's dryest elements too much remained for Positivists, and so on.

I don't often trouble you with my own papers; but if you have time to run through the accompanying three, you will see, I hope with Branford, Arthur Thomson and others, we are getting towards clearness and even policy. The general idea of these papers (marked I. II. III) is that:

I – We have constantly to be re-surveying our world and interpreting it, at once in science and in Philosophy, both of nature and of man – ("Voir" and "Savoir" – even "prevoir" – (Pro-Synthesis).

II – To discern this as definitely from Urban to Rustic, mechanical to vital, hence renewal of social feeling and thought towards action – "Penser pour Agir!"

III – to coordinate our action, as Social Transition, active and thoughtful, together by turns.

We have thus to get beyond our Outlook Tower, telescope, botanic gardens and geologic, historic chateau etc. and towards fuller utilisation of vital and spiritual outlook, and constructive and creative expression, such as are yours.

As example: Bose (I mean Prof. of Philosophy) is welcome here – and the more since striving to correlate Indian and European philosophy. Here is the ideal link; between our Scots College, with its garden literally "peripatetic" – since its walks and terraces are being adjusted to illustrate the viewpoints of the west from Greeks onwards to today; and we are puzzling now over how to do the like for Indian College, now rising fast.

Thus towards a higher and fuller outlook than either alone. (Interesting that my Edinburgh architectural partner, without suggestion from me, has sketched Asoke's pillar on its own corner Tower!)

So, pray, send Bose a message of encouragement towards this unification of philosophies; it is sure to help him.

Yours always

P. Geddes

P.S.

I do not now ask you; but when you come, I trust you may see advantage in the widening cooperation I am beginning to organise with kindred living groups and struggling undertakings in Edinburgh and London, etc. and in Paris, Brussels and Geneva, etc. as with corresponding beginnings in America too.

We have all too long been struggling separately, and so far well: yet is it not time also to be joining hands across the world, and expressing ourselves – each in our own regional conditions and ways, as in movement – and this of many kinds.

You, who read musical notations as well as printed and verbal, will in a few minutes see the sense of my two diagrams (pages 112-123). Thus when you look at both together, (hence intervening pages pinned out of the way) you will see their symmetric contrast – from mechanistic, on left, to vital, on right – (with the main succession in each case with blacker edges, and their accompaniments lighter.)

Thus, either I am quite mad, or I have got the social situation a stage clearer than hitherto – and this both as regards the Mechanical Age, with its too illusory progress, and real decadence, and the incipient Revivance: and each with its main elements – hence changes towards better things more intelligibly indicated and related.

P. G.

INDIAN COLLEGE
PLAN DES QUATRE SEIGNEURS
MONTPELLIER[143]

19 March 1930

Dear Tagore

I am writing to Elmhirst to ask him to tell me of your plans of approaching journey to Europe for your Oxford Lectures etc; so you need not trouble to reply to this. But I am sure you will permit me to say how much we are looking forward to your promised visit here – in course of which we hope you will perform the simple ceremony of laying our Memorial Stone – (for it can no longer be called "foundation stone", since this first block of Indian College is now in part two storeys high, and in part being finished as three storeys). It is the gift of the Sir Ratan Tata Trustees, and consists mainly of large library with gallery, and study-room, above the future dining-room; but Advani will have to return to Bombay in autumn to find the funds to build the rest – the rooms for students. These will be meantime accommodated as *hitherto* in the Scots College, now trebled, by my wife's help. I am glad to say that besides the Havells, we shall have other tutorial colleagues, in fact, quite a group. And I am

---

[143] Indian College letterhead.

pleased to tell you that one of these is my first student-assistant of more than 40 years ago, who – (after a career of wider range than mine as to students' hall of residence, University Settlement in Manchester, and positively colossal city and village improvements in Manchester, Yorkshire and Leeds, and for last 8 years in rebuilding war-ruined villages in Northern France) – has now retired, and come back here to help me on longer scale than of old. I tell you this, because I am sure it will encourage you in the expectation of having your own work thus strengthened and carried on by some of your own old Santiniketan boys and students, as they mature in their own turn also.

When you come, I hope you will give us a brief (but none the less vital!) address:– and if you will allow me further, I transmit the invitation of many members of the University here to speak of them. (say next day). A good many here understand English, and for others the Professor of English will give an excellent summary-translation in French. (But of course if you dread fatigue – we can let you off with one talk!)

But to continue my requests – may I also express – again on behalf of University and City people alike their very earnest desire to have a visit and word from you at Edinburgh, after your Oxford lectures are over? People will come not only from Glasgow, but from far further over Scotland to hear you: and at this juncture – (if wider discussion of "What's wrong with Scotland!" than ever before) you will have a very open-minded and receptive audience – and help us all accordingly!

Pardon these many demands! And believe me as ever cordially, loyally and affectionately yours

P. Geddes

60 Rue St Lazare
Trinité
Paris

5 April 1930.

My dear Geddes,

Confirming my letter of April 1st. I have just learnt that Tagore is staying at the Villa Kahn, Cap Martin, and I am told will be there till the end of the month. The "Amis de la Paix" would like to have him at their May lunch, which we would fix, if it would suit him, for Saturday the 10th of that month, when we should be able to have Lord Tyrrell and probably M. ardieu[144], and other French statesmen.

I propose to have on the same occasion the chief French poet, Paul Valery, brother of your Montpellier friend and, if he approves, H.G. Wells.

The "Amitiés Internationales", with which the "Amis" are affiliated, would like to hear him at the Institut of "Cooperation Intellectuelle", and on that occasion would have a large attendance of his admirers, British and French and other resident in Paris. The nationalists-reactionaries would no doubt like to enlist him as an enemy of England, but I am sure there is no more earnest votary for peace than a man who is one of the glories of the British civilisations.

We have just given a warm welcome to Emil Ludwig and his wife (Scotch on her Mother's side, by the way,) and that we shall give to Tagore will outshine it, for he represents not one country but civilisation common to all cultured races.

Tagore is no doubt staying at the Cap Martin residence of Kahn, of the "Tour du Monde", whose work for peace has won the respect of all advocates of international conciliation.

---

[144] The first letter of this name is not clear.

Of course we shall write and invite him and feel honoured if he would be one of your guests.

Hoping to hear from you shortly,
and with kindest regards,
Ever your old friend,
Thomas Barclay[145]

Villa Danure
Cap Martin
12 April 1930

Dear Geddes

I am sure I shall have time to come to you by the end of this month. I have decided to accept Sir Thomas Barclay's invitation though I am puzzled at the delusion of the people who think that I can make speeches having done nothing to deserve such uncomfortable reputation.

Cordially Yours

Rabindranath Tagore

---

[145] The letter is typed. There is a hand-written note at the top of the letter saying, 'From Sir Thomas Barclay – Law Offices'. At the bottom of the letter, there is another hand-written note which says, 'Sir Thomas is blind, hence a somewhat vague signature', which is then signed 'P.G.'

Cap Martin
19 April 1930

My dear Geddes,

Gurudev wished intensely not to disappoint you and it was with the greatest reluctance that we persuaded him not to undertake another journey at this very critical time when his heart-trouble has again become evident, and he has felt pains all over his chest which the doctor who is with him takes seriously. I consulted the doctor about it knowing what a terrible disappointment it would be to you, but he was dead against it; and the very night after the decision was taken the pains increased and Gurudev himself realised that it would be impossible. The Hibbert Lectures are before him and he has cancelled all engagements before that time. I am afraid it is still doubtful if he will have strength to get through.

I should have come myself to see you and the College, but Gurudev leaves today and I understand that it is your Easter holiday time and your students will be away. If it is possible to come later in the year I will certainly do so. Will you give my kindest remembrances to Advani?

Yours very sincerely

C.F. Andrews

Villa Danure
Cap Martin
20 April 1930

Dear Dr. Geddes,

I am writing this letter to you claiming your forgiveness for not allowing Sir. Rabindranath Tagore to make a journey to Montpellier on his way to Paris. I am his medical adviser and I feel greatly anxious about his state of health. I am certain that he should not strain himself in the least and risk a serious breakdown before he is ready for the Oxford lecture. Night before last, he had a sudden relapse of his weakness and though he has got over it, it is a warning which he must take seriously.

All his arrangements in Paris and in other places must be cancelled except the Hibbert lectures which cannot be avoided.

I have great admiration for your work and your personality and it is only my sense of duty which has compelled me to prevent him from attending your ceremony and taking part in it.

I remain

Yours sincerely

S.N. Chaudhuri. Capt. IMS (rtd)
M.R.C.S, L.R.C.P. Lond.
(Ballygunj – Calcutta).

Cap. Martin
20 April 1930

Dear Geddes,

You know I was ready to come to you about the end of this month but suddenly I had a bad attack of pain in the chest which according to our doctor is a symptom that must not be neglected. It compels me to cancel all my engagements in order to keep myself fit for the last one which is the Hibbert lecture. I feel extremely sorry but I know that you will sympathise with me and readily absolve me from promise.

Cordially Yours

Rabindranath Tagore[146]

---

[146] This letter is written in a very unsteady hand.

Dear Tagore,

It has grieved me sorely to hear of your illness and the interruption of your splendid progress through the world, which despite all drawbacks, ever widening, quickening, awakening to your message.

May it perhaps encourage you, if I put the idea of some of us working sociologists – which inspires Branford and my books especially – that of understanding the present *i.e.* still predominantly but <u>changing</u> Industrial Age? Well, when we were young, even anthropologists still talked of the "Stone Age" – the first industrial age – of flint implements. But in this they long ago learned to distinguish two main periods – the old and the (for it) new – a Paleolithic and Neo-lithic respectively – and now, in France especially, they have clearly worked out distinct periods of advance with each). But enough for us these two – the Paleolithic people essentially hunters and (fisherwomen) and root and fruit gatherers, but the finer and truer special civilization that goes with that – in short thus founding the older elements of our civilization of today – albeit interrupted by bronze, and iron, with their increasingly furious perturbations and interruptions through War, and with formation of "States" accordingly.

This contrast clearly realized, as well as established by advancing science, considers its modern applications. There is not one "Industrial Age" of machinery, of mammon and war, which awoke Ruskin's protest, and both his [illegible] as it sometimes well nigh has yours, mine too and many too. This age has also two forms – old and new – <u>Paleotechnic</u> and <u>Neotechnic</u>.

The former, characterized by getting up coal (any how) to get up steam (any how) to sell them (any how) to clothe and breed more cheap people (any how), and to spread them by railways and ships into the empires and for profit (any how), to be *stimulated* by "successful" – in gold terms (any how) – has thus had Progress for its Politics and "Political Economy" for its

---

[147] This letter has no date on it. It was probably written after 20 April 1930, when Geddes learnt of Tagore's illness. There is a very rough draft on top of which is scribbled in Geddes' hand '(not yet sent)'. One hopes it was sent as it reiterates Geddes' ideas of the two broad divisions of men – the Neolithic and the Paleolithic – which accounts for the present world situation. The sentences are sometimes not fully framed, as the whole reads as notes for a letter rather than a final copy.

dogma and the extinguished Industrial Hells of Britain and America, and Bombay too for result – War and anarchies as essential condition.

The latter clearly now incipient science as much with minor successes [illegible] victory – is of [illegible] energies of nature and its centralism by electricity with its decentralisation and thus by dirt, soil etc. by cleanliness of all. And to produce increasingly good things. Contrast the debased Wembly Exhibition (though even that had better elements) with the present Paris one, in which this Neolithic age has its cleared presentment yet, incomplete though that still be). Thus towards production for vital uses, expressed with art, helped by science – now no longer mechanical but vital (and evolutionary in truer sense than the conventionally deemed, witness Bergson. Thus too regional cultures renewing – as your in Bengal, as Zionists here, as *Plunkett* in Ireland and some of us in Scotland too – and so on – and increasingly in France, Spain etc. Thus for the People in renewing old sense – in which you write their [illegible].

And thus with Mammon becoming exorcised – by the "good job" of social use and service – true crafts and arts and faith again as old as Regional Development *i.e.* Agriculture, Forestry etc. Thus little bits of Cosmos re-appearing as yourself, and other sane workers – as making here too – in which it is a pleasure to plan.

So while all true spirits have been jarred by the lower mechanical mammon and war – and above all necessarily you poets – so it is peculiarly an age for you to rejoice with, and lead us in song (from craft-song to soul-song is after all not so far).

For what the old prophets protested against the evils of the lower knowledge (mammon, mechanistic life, thought and wars). But what is it that the great religions expressed and systematised[148]? Was it not just what we now call the psychological and vital. So these too <u>practically</u>, or Etho-polity, as Psycho-organics, and as Eu-technics and thus these unified as Religion. In these senses are sciences – as per Victor Branford's "Science and Sanctity", "Living religions" etc. is re-religious and is making towards Re-Religion.[149]

---

[148] This is one of Geddes' abbreviations written as 'systd.'
[149] The draft is unfinished.

Enclos.[150] *(sic)*
C/o L.K.E., Dartington, Totnes, Devon
10 July 1930

Dear Amiya Babu,

It was a great pleasure to hear from you. After some alarums? I made the excursion here, and had 2 or 3 days with the Bard and have advanced to a stage whereby <u>with</u> your help, I should be able to publish the songs as I wish. (Need I say what a profound pleasure it has been to meet my friend Gurudeva again? and Rathi and Pratima Devi, and Lal?)

In answer to your kind messages. I should have great pleasure in meeting again, believe me, and in meeting your wife. I shall be here for 1 or 2 weeks, then in (or near) London as I want to finish Bengal, as thesis and book. I go North about September. Do let me know if you're to be in or near London. I should be glad to talk over Bengal and hear what you feel needs saying to strengthen the links of understanding, as you said, and break down barriers.

Yours sincerely

Arthur Geddes.

14.7.30. P.S. I realise after writing out the list that transliteration of 16 songs, – translation of 7 of these, will be a big job and I know you have plenty to do yourself. Perhaps, if you've time to do some, and find some one to help me with others, – those for which you have no time. It would be nice to get the book ready for the poetic translator, as soon as may be – beginning with a few. If you could send me, first the transliterations of those for which I have translations, we could start…

A G.

---

[150] What the enclosure might have been, is not apparent.

C/o L.K. Elmhirst

Dartington Hall,

Totnes, Devon

13 July 1930.

Dear Mr. Bake,

It is a pleasure to know that you have tackled the great work of noting Dr. Tagore's songs: a difficult but fine task. I owe you many apologies for not having answered your kind letter of 16.2.28 (I think it was): some of the MS was lost and various delays to my work made me very behind hand with this and other things I wished to do. I have just had 3 days with Dr. Tagore and we have gone over a number of songs: herewith is the best of those noted. I've noted enough of the airs to identify them by.

Will you tell me <u>which</u>, if any of those you've noted? I might also include some noted by Benoit ('Inde is now Amar').

I am writing to *her*, Amiya Chakravarty (asking him to forward this for me) and asking him to let me have the <u>words</u> and translated. I have to have these translated in verse by a friend so that the songs could be sung in English. (the Poet had suggested my trying this too – but success is uncertain).

I wonder if you have been in touch with Philippe Stern, *(sic)* (90 Boulevard Malesherbes, Paris) of the Ecole des Hautes Etudes, Sorbornne, who is interested in the publication of Oriental music, and offered to help with the publication of these. I did not accept, feeling that, as <u>English</u> is the European language spoken in India, and her closest [illegible] is with Britain and USA that these songs should first be published in English. Phil Sterne *(sic)* however is a good, careful man who is making a genuinely scientific study of Oriental music. His official notations for special features of Oriental music would be worth adopting. I hope that you will not keep my letter so long unanswered as I have kept yours.

Yours sincerely

Arthur Geddes

Dear Gurudeva,

It is so long since I have written that you may well wonder what has become of me, and of what I hoped to complete for you. Instead of being able to say today (as I should so dearly like to) that any share of the task is done, I come to ask if you will honour the memory of your friend, my father, by giving your name to the accompanying letter to the Principal. If so, will you "Air Mail" your consent, to me, as the Outlook Tower Committee have asked me to write to you.

I wish you could meet my wife, she would dearly love to know you.

And now as to the Songs – your songs, – I've tried one or two translators in vain; but one more has promised to try, and I'm sending some of the verses and tunes and I'm to try playing them over to her. Since I saw you I did get literal, prose translations, but not yet the singable translations I hope for.

It's true that I've not pushed the matter as I hoped to, ... my Professor has helped me at the two geographical books *(sic)* I've now almost finished "Bengal" and the "Western Isles of Lewis and Harris". One interruption to these I must confess – the "Spirit of the Tartan" (of which I'd like to send you a note later, for it would never have been written but for seeing and hearing the song Dramas for "Sacrifice" and the "Dark Chamber" – and "Spring Tune".

Well, if you can Air Mail the word "Yes", I shall be grateful – and all of us deeply glad.

With homage and affectionate greeting to all from

Arthur[151]

---

[151] The end of the letter, after 'Sacrifice', is continued in the left-hand margin.

24 November 1934

Dear Arthur,

It was nice to get your letter and have your news. I heartily approve of the project of a suitable memorial to your father and I gladly give my name as a signatory to the appeal.

With affectionate greetings to all of you,

Yours sincerely

Rabindranath Tagore[152]

Arthur Geddes Esq.,
Geographical Department,
The University,
Edinburgh

---

[152] The signature, including the parenthetical information, is hand-written, signed by Tagore, in what otherwise is a typed letter, which is quite uncharacteristic of Tagore.

Dear Gurudeva,

It was a great pleasure to receive, this morning, your warm letter and your acceptance of our request to sign the memorial to carry on my father's work. (I have sent it on to the Secretary). We <u>value</u> it.

Bengal is daily (almost hourly) in my thoughts and I wish that, someday, I might re-visit India, and Bengal. As I said, my study of Bengal is nearing completion. Further, I've a capable assistant helping with preparatory maps of India's population as a basis for my promised work on India. Of course India will only be a reconnaissance but when that is made the visit to India would show me so much that I did not see (for lack of eyes!) when I was there last, and that no one has described.

"<u>Bengal</u>" is on my own plan (and will be my own venture). "India" is to be written for a good series (Harrap) but I think the recommendation of their Geographical editor (Prof. Rudmose[153] Brown) would have pleased you – "Other books describe India as the European sees it, and the "Commercial geographies" written up to now too often show how money is made out of India —. Let's have something that tries to show how the ryot [peasant], and the citizen, see their country, and how they make their life there, and might make a better one!"

I've often thought of your scheme of "travelling geographers", of a travelling <u>school</u> (or College) through India, and how immensely interesting it would be to join it! You said (when Andrews pled with you to go strong for political unity of India) "If we cannot win our blood, we will not spill it together." Perhaps the first step is to mix minds – as you do at

---

[153] In the hand-written letter, the name looks like 'Ron', but is spelt out in the typed letter and the 'ud' are written over the two second letters by hand.

Santiniketan somewhat (though not many come from other provinces)[154], and beyond that, to send an embassy of learners through the land! How much could they see, learn and understand, take with them and bring!

With thanks once more,

and warm affection

Arthur[155]

---

[154] In Arthur's hand-written letter, this section is in brackets, while in the typed copy of it, it is within two dashes.

[155] On top of the typed copy, there is a hand-written note saying, 'In case my letter's not legible, my wife has a typed …'. The end is cut off in the photocopy of the typed copy.

The eternal dream
    is borne on the wings of ageless Light
    that rends the veil of the vague
        and goes across time
    weaving ceaseless patterns of Being.

The mystery remains dumb,
    the meanings of this pilgrimage,
    the endless adventure of existence
whose rush along the sky
    flames up innumerable rings of paths,
till at last knowledge gleams out from the dusk
        in the infinity of human spirit,
and in the dim lighted dawn
she speechlessly gazes through the break in the mist
    at the vision of Life and of Love
rising from the tumult of profound pain and joy.

Santiniketan
16 September 1929

(composed for the Opening Day Celebrations of the Indian College, Montpellier, France)

From: Das, Sisir Kumar, ed., *The English Writings of Rabindranath Tagore*, (1996) Volume Three, p. 86.

Poem by Tagore written shortly after the death of Patrick Geddes
(English version overleaf)

The night has ended.
Put out the light of the lamp
of thine own narrow corner
smudged with smoke.
The great morning which is for all
appears in the East.
Let its light reveal us
to each other
who walk on
the same
path of pilgrimage.

Baghdad, May 24, 1932

Bibliography

Boardman, Philip *Patrick Geddes: Maker of the Future*, Introduction by Lewis Mumford (Chapel Hill: The University of North Carolina Press, 1944).

Boardman, Philip *The World of Patrick Geddes: Biologist, Town Planner, Re-educator, Peace Warrior* (London: Routledge, 1978).

Chaudhuri, Nirad C. *The Autobiography of an Unknown Indian*, 1951 (Bombay: Jaico Publishing House, 3rd impression, 1969).

Das, Sisir Kumar ed. *The English Writings of Rabindranath Tagore: A Miscellany* (New Delhi: Rabindra-Bhavana, Sahitya Akademy, 1996, Vol Three).

Defries, Amelia *The Interpreter Geddes: The Man and the Gospel*, Introduction by Israel Zangwill (London: George Routledge and Sons Ltd., 1927).

Desai, Anita. 'Re-reading Tagore' in *Journal of Commonwealth Literature*, 29/1, 1994.

Dutta, Krishma and Robinson, Andrew *Rabindranath Tagore: The Myriad-Minded Man* (Bloomsbury, 1995).

Dutta, Krishma and Robinson, Andrew *Rabindranath Tagore: An Anthology* (Picador, 1997).

Fischer, Louis *The Life of Mahatma Gandhi*, (London: Granada, 1951).

Geddes, Arthur 'Two Friends: Rabindranath Tagore and Patrick Geddes' in *Annual Journal of Architecture, Structure and Planning*, 1961.

Geddes, Patrick *An Indian Pioneer: The Life and Work of Sir J.C. Bose*, 1920 (New Delhi and Madras: Asia Educational Services, 2000).

Geddes, Patrick 'Education and Reconstruction: A Review' in *Visva-Bharati Quarterly, April* (Bengali: Vaisakh, 1331, 1924).

Kabir, Humayun *Towards Universal Man: Rabindranath Tagore* (London: Asia Publishing House, 1961).

Kitchen, Paddy *A Most Unsettling Person* (London: Victor Gollancz Ltd., 1975).

Kripalani, Krishna *Rabindranath Tagore: A Biography* (New York: Grove Press Inc., 1962).

Macdonald, Murdo 'Patrick Geddes – Educator, Ecologist, Visual Thinker' in *Edinburgh Review*, Issue 88, Summer, 1992.

Mairet, Philip *Pioneer in Sociology: The Life and Letters of Patrick Geddes* (London: Lund Humphries, 1957).

Meller, Helen *Patrick Geddes: Social Evolutionist and City Planner* (London and New York: Routledge, 1990).

Novak, Frank G. ed. with Introduction *Lewis Mumford and Patrick Geddes: The Correspondence* (London and New York: Routledge, 1995).

Stalley, Marshall ed. with Introduction *Patrick Geddes: Spokesman for Man and the Environment: A Selection* (New Brunswick, New Jersey: Rutgers University Press, 1972).

Tagore, Rabindranath *Reminiscences*, 1917 (Madras: Macmillan, rpt. 1971).

Tagore, Rabindranath 'Universities' in *The Modern Review*, April 1919, Vol. XXV, No. 1.

Tagore, Rabindranath *The Visva-Bharati Quarterly*, October (Bengali: Kartic, 1331, 1924).

Index